EAGLE MAN

EAGLE MAN

Charles L. Broley's Field
Adventures with American Eagles
by Myrtle Jeanne Broley

PELLEGRINI & CUDAHY • PUBLISHERS
NEW YORK

PRINTED IN THE UNITED STATES OF AMERICA

PUBLISHED SIMULTANEOUSLY IN CANADA BY

GEORGE J. MCLEOD, LTD.

To Richard H. Pough

Contents

[vii]

Contents

List of Illustrations

The Eagle

He clasps the crag with crooked hands,
Close to the sun in lonely lands,
Ringed with the azure world, he stands.

The wrinkled sea beneath him crawls,
He watches from the mountain walls,
And like a thunderbolt he falls.

Alfred, Lord Tennyson

Charles L. Broley

He climbs the pine with skilful hands,
Close to the sun in lovely lands,
To meet the stately bird he bands.

The Voice of Science to him calls:
His daring hobby never palls—
And—glad we are—he never falls.

F. Beacon Rich
PRESIDENT, HALIFAX RIVER BIRD CLUB
DAYTONA BEACH, FLORIDA

Introduction

No HISTORY of bird-watching in North America will be complete without a section devoted to the work of Charles L. Broley.

This Canadian ex-banker who took up eagle-banding on his retirement and who has continued his strenuous and not undangerous hobby into his seventies, is one of the most colorful—and valuable—of modern bird-men.

To watch him string his rope ladders and work his way up some ancient tree toward the crowning mass of an eagle's nest—as I once did on the Kissimmee Prairie of Florida—is to share vicariously in an adventure that is long remembered.

But there is always a hard core of invaluable purpose in Broley's avocation. Science benefits from the risks he takes. So far, he has placed numbered aluminum bands on more than 1200 bald eagles. This is well over a dozen times the number banded by all other ornithologists put together.

Out of his work new facts have come to light about the bird that is the national emblem of the United States. Bald eagles are long-lived birds. So bands he has placed on the legs of nestlings may well continue to provide a harvest of facts for a generation to come.

Myrtle J. Broley has shared in many of the field ventures of her husband. She is best equipped of all to tell the story of his work. In *Eagle Man*, she has done it effectively and simply, in a style that precisely fits the subject.

All those who have met Broley, read of his exploits, or heard him lecture will be indebted to this book for its mass of background material on his earlier life and the anecdotes stressing the outstanding characteristics of his personality: his sense of humor, his courage, his enthusiasm.

In her book, Mrs. Broley has set down a great deal of information about eagles. She has also stressed the need for protection for the national bird, a conservation goal that the work of Charles L. Broley has done most to further.

Eagle Man is a book of solid worth, a source book filled with facts. It is also a warm, human story of a remarkable man whose achievements are an inspiration to all. Appropriately the book is dedicated to Richard H. Pough, Curator of Conservation at the American Museum of Natural History, whose suggestion led Broley into this great adventure of his life.

Edwin Way Teale

EAGLE MAN

CHAPTER ONE

How It All Began

BANDING YOUNG bald eagles seems an odd hobby for a man to take up after retiring, but that is what Charles Lavelle Broley did and he has made a success of it.

For many years he was a staid banker who saw few eagles except those on bills or coins, although he did try to see the real ones whenever possible.

He is slightly built, wiry, five feet nine and a half, and at seventy-one does not look anywhere near his age. He can tramp, climb, or pack in gear with the best of them and frequently is quite fresh when younger men are tired out with long hikes. When he is introduced, as very often happens, as "the bald-headed eagle man," he is much amused for he is, in truth, as devoid of hair on his scalp as many people believe this bird to be, not realizing that in early English "bald" meant white as well as bare. In old Anglo-Saxon, "Beald" was the word for courageous or bold and this, too, might have been given to our bird in spite of what some writers have said. Charlie's blue eyes are very keen, and he might almost be said to have the proverbial eagle's eye.

[3]

His agility when climbing trees amazes everyone, especially those who "fall with every step you take," as one woman watching him ascend to a very high nest said.

He has worked out his method very carefully, however, and does not take risks, even though at times the whole thing appears very hazardous.

For a number of years before retiring he had concentrated on studying, during off days and holidays, waterfowl in Manitoba, a favorite spot for them in spring and summer as well as early fall. About April tenth or so the waves of snow and blue geese would arrive to rest up on the flooded meadows between Winnipeg and Portage la Prairie before starting their long flight to their nesting grounds in Baffin Land. There were many Canada geese around, too, but the other flocks were so vast, so spectacular, that the Canadas attracted much less attention.

Charlie was the first of the naturalists around there to observe that these great gaggles had moved over from Whitewater Lake, fast drying up, to the region between Lake Winnipeg and Lake Manitoba. All his holidays and most Sundays were spent out studying them and any other birds, of course, that happened to be in the vicinity.

His hours in the field there helped to curb illegal shooting, for he was instrumental in having a number of men, among them a game warden, fined and deprived of their guns for killing snow geese in the spring.

When the flocks of wavies, as they are called, left with the strong south winds of early May—or in milder springs, late April—he turned his attention to the resident waterfowl, watching the fast flying skeins of ducks in mating flights, searching out nests so that he could photograph them and study their composition and the down with which they were lined.

I remember one trip we made when Jeanne, our daughter, was about five. She was keenly interested in wild life even at that age, and her father would carry her in to see a red-head duck's beautiful basket and eggs built in rushes amidst water that was knee high for him, or to show her the canvasback's nest with its down so much darker than that of its near relative.

On this trip Charlie had walked down along the little creek on which we were camped while Jeanne got herself ready for bed. I was sitting near by, giving advice or help from time to time, when suddenly I noticed Charlie throw something and then run back like mad.

Turning around, he went back a little way, threw something, and tore off again. When he had repeated these actions several times, I had to find out what he was doing and got out my binoculars. A white-striped skunk or "woods kitty" had been ambling along the edge of the water towards us, and he was trying to persuade it to go in the other direction. He was successful, too, but I still laugh when I think how peculiar his actions looked from where I sat.

He searched out and studied the nests of all the wild ducks to be found on the prairies and could tell, with very little hesitation, to which species a nest belonged even when he had not seen the female leave. Little Ruddy had him fooled for quite awhile. He would see the males on a slough but apparently they called the females off, for he was unable to flush them. No sign of a nest rewarded his searchings either, except for one with very large eggs. He was sure this could not be Mistress Ruddy's; after all, she is one of the smallest of our wild ducks and would not have an egg larger than that of the canvasback. The mystery intrigued him and at last he managed to see the owner of the nest leaving. She was indeed a tiny female Ruddy.

These beautiful white eggs hatch dark little ducklings which are most precocious. They can dive and swim before they are dry from the shell.

Charlie was never so hurried that he could not take time to talk a little about conservation to the people he met, especially the country lads. Near a marsh one day, he saw a boy sauntering along, and stopped to ask if he knew of any nests near by.

"Flushed a mallard back in that field," he answered. "She had nine eggs."

"Did you cover them up?" Charlie asked. Wild ducks make a mat of grass stems and fine roots mixed with down plucked from their breast and, when they have time to do so, pull this over their eggs before leaving them. This both protects the eggs from the sun or from chilling and also hides them from sight. Anyone finding a nest uncovered should try to put this blanket in place to foil crows and other enemies.

The boy looked quite crestfallen when he admitted he had not bothered, and Charlie suggested going back with him to see if all was well. Though only a short time had elapsed, they were too late. A sharp-eyed crow had seen the

boy stop to look at the nest and flown over on his departure. When Charlie and the lad arrived, he had almost
finished a meal of duck eggs.

Most boys are glad to learn facts about nature and Charlie enlisted a great many of the ones he met in the rural
districts in the ranks of nature lovers and conservationists.

On a trip to Selkirk, at the foot of Lake Winnipeg, he
made an astonishing record. In a little pool of water, almost surrounded by reeds, he saw a heron standing. For
half an hour we watched it and studied every marking.
Size, coloring, the white line down the throat, there was no
question about it, especially after a bittern slipped quietly
in beside it so that we could more accurately gauge the
length. This was a Louisiana heron, a bird of the South and
never before, nor since, reported in Manitoba or indeed in
Canada. Young herons have a habit of wandering far
afield, though, as may be seen by the arrival of a number
of young egrets in northern localities each summer. No
doubt other Louisiana herons may have wandered up but
have not been sighted. At any rate, though he might have
done so, he did not shoot the lovely creature, preferring a
live bird to a definite record. All ornithologists who know
his integrity and careful identification give it to him as a
sight record anyway.

The first avocets to wander into Manitoba when their
alkaline ponds in Alberta and Saskatchewan were dried up
during the drought were discovered by him. I can well
recall the day of this find. My parents lived in Portage la
Prairie, only about fifteen miles from Lake Manitoba. We

had gone home for a week end and Charlie had, at once, gone to a creek not far from the lake to see if there was anything unusual around.

When he returned to Mother's I went to meet him and knew by his beaming face that he had seen something exciting.

"You can't guess what I saw!" he cried.

Now neither of us had mentioned avocets for months, so when I said, "Not an avocet?" he looked quite surprised but assured me that he had indeed seen this lovely, long-legged bird. Of course I had to go out at once to revel in its black, white and pink plumage, so picturesque with those blue legs. Later I found the first nest reported for Manitoba. It was in the area where Charlie had shown me my first one of these birds, and I must confess that if I had not been so lazy I would not have found it. While he searched the grassy places where the books said nests would be most likely, I went to sit by the car, for it was a very hot day. Noticing an avocet fly over the muddy edge of the creek, squat, then act as if pushing eggs about and settle down, I walked over. She rose with a cry as I drew near. I yelled for Charlie to see what I had found, a cup-like depression in the mud with four elongated buffy eggs. Of course he proceeded to find several other nests near by, but I had found the first one!

Another first for him was the dickcissel which came into Manitoba about this same time. This bird, like a miniature meadowlark, is fairly rare in Canada, especially on the prairies, but that year a nesting colony was located after Charlie had spotted this arrival.

It was hard to say whether he was just lucky or if it was because he did spend so much of his time in the field. At any rate, when a rare bird turned up in Manitoba he was usually the first to see it. He found a flock of Hudsonian godwits which passed through each spring and on one memorable autumn day we saw a whooping crane, the large white one that is now reduced in numbers to about thirty in all. Naturalists are trying so hard to enlarge the flock but have had little success so far. Our crane was leading a flock of sandhills, smaller brown cranes of the same family.

Possibly because of this fortunate sight, Charlie was asked a few years ago to try to find some nests of the whooping crane in northern Canada. The Audubon Association planned to have men guard these and the birds to insure safe nesting. While he did organize a complete coverage of the area by radio, newspaper, and other means of communication, he felt he could not do the field work at that time as we were living in Ontario then. A few authentic records for other years were sent in but no nests were found that season.

The bitter cold of western Canadian winters did not keep him from his trips to the country. He enjoyed the yearly arrival of the big snowy owls and hunted out their pellets atop strawstacks to send to scientists interested in finding out on what these birds fed. The hundreds of snow bunting, sweeping across the snow-covered plains like large brown and white butterflies delighted him, and the winter that brought an influx of hawk owls from the far north was a banner one.

Regularly he took a Christmas census, walking miles to glimpse as many species as possible. On one blustery day when the thermometer was down around forty below he covered a great many miles, driving from place to place, then tramping in to where birds should have been. He was out from nine in the morning until late afternoon and his total count was one chickadee! Winnipeg's record was not on the list that year, and we felt it should have been included if only to show the effect of a cold, stormy day.

He has some good records for Ontario also. He and Jeanne located a nesting colony of prairie warblers on Devil Lake, not far from our island. He also found the nest of the goshawk—but more about that later.

In 1938, at the age of fifty-eight, he decided to retire from his position as Manager of the Corydon Avenue Branch of the Bank of Montreal in Winnipeg. He thought he would like a little more time for bird study before he became too old to enjoy it. First though, with Jeanne and me, he took a trip to the British Isles, France, Portugal, and the Canary Islands. We visited museums, saw the famous egg collected by Edward Wilson at the South Pole when he took the "Worst Journey in the World" to find the nesting place of the emperor penguin. Wherever we went he was watching for birds. On the cruise ship, steaming towards Madeira, a tiny warbler we were unable to identify landed aboard, too weary to flutter further. Charlie gave it water and found a safe shelter for it. After some time it winged away again.

On our return to Canada, we decided to attend a meeting of the American Ornithologists' Union in Washington on our way to spend the winter months in Florida. Little did Charlie think that this was to be a turning point in his life.

For some time he had been corresponding with Richard Pough of New York, who was very much interested in the protection of birds of prey as well as in seeing that the trade in feathers was stopped. At these sessions the two men met and a lasting friendship was the result.

"How about getting someone to band some bald eagles while you are in Florida?" Dick asked one day. "Couldn't you find some boy who might do it under your supervision?"

"Are there many bald eagles in Florida?" Charlie countered.

Dick told him what he knew about the eagle population there. "You see," he added, "too many of these fine birds are being shot. We'd like to put a stop to that. Like to find out more about them, also; what they feed on, the amount of predation, and so forth. It's a good way to popularize our national emblem, also, and give it publicity at this troubled time."

Charlie promised to have a try at doing this, although he intimated that his own climbing days were over. "Used to be able to shinny up a tree with anyone," he shrugged. "Guess such days are past. I'll keep my feet on the ground now. Someone else can have my share of climbing."

Which just proves how little he knew what was ahead of him.

Dick gave him four bands and the accompanying cards to be filled out, wished him luck in the project, and assured him that he'd be happy to send a few more bands if he should need them.

Not realizing it, Charlie had embarked on the work that was to make his name known throughout Canada, the United States, and Great Britain, to add much to the knowledge about the American bald eagle, and even to add a few words and phrases to the English language such as "Do a Broley" for getting up a tree with the aid of ropes as he does.

Wherever he bands or lectures he enlists new friends for these birds he loves. They help in guarding nests and in gathering information as to dates or feeding habits. He was instrumental in having the collecting of eagle eggs stopped in Florida and it was greatly due to his work that such a heavy fine was imposed for shooting one of these magnificent and regal birds.

CHAPTER TWO

Florida

IT IS not surprising that Charles Broley should have planned to spend his winters, after retirement, in Florida. For over a century and a half this long, narrow peninsula jutting southward into the tropics has been a Mecca for scientists of all kinds and for ornithologists especially. It is a natural flyway for a great many migrating birds, both spring and fall. That many decide, very wisely, to stay right there and travel no more we may be certain, for its multitude of freshwater lakes and ponds, its tidal lagoons and salt water marshes, make it an ideal site for most kinds of waterfowl, shore birds, and swamp lovers while its excellent climate attracts birds of tree and bush.

The waters about are full of food for terns, gulls, cormorants, and skimmers. Pelicans, with their waddling, absurd gait ashore, thrill observers when they sail or soar overhead or dive after fish with a tremendous splash into the deep blue waters of gulf or bay. Windy days bring the storm bird—the graceful man-o'-war bird—which for its weight has the longest wings of any bird alive and so is able to rise and soar on the slightest breeze and is thought to be a harbinger of bad weather. Bush and thicket swarm with mocking birds, cardinals, warblers, and other brightly colored little fellows.

By dugout canoe many of the first human visitors reached Florida. Later came the colorful Spanish galleons and pirate vessels. Warships of many nations have called there, and many ships have been sunk on reefs that still carry the name of the unlucky craft. Now airplanes, trains, fine cruisers, as well as automobiles by the thousands, bring the many who travel south to enjoy summer in January. Naturalists enjoy meeting up again with the birds that left their localities in September and October, or study and photograph species that do not go further north. It is indeed a bird-lover's paradise.

When we read about traveling in Florida a hundred years ago, we are surprised that any birds remain. The common entrance to central and southern Florida was by steamboat on the St. John's River to Lake Monroe and then a short trip overland to Indian River or some comparable spot. Trees with their lovely drapery of Spanish moss, like soft curtains blowing in the breeze, were all along the banks and in places arched completely over the water. Crocodiles and turtles sunned themselves on the shore, waterfowl of every kind swam or fed busily, merely moving out of the way for the noisy, big structure coming in beside them. Pink clouds of roseate spoonbills, contrasting so beautifully with pure white egrets and herons, flew above the trees or fed on muddy flats, their greenish, spatulate beaks so clumsy looking. White blossoms of ibises enlivened the dark foliage and countless hawks, kites, and eagles filled the air. The very thought fills us with a deep resentment against the cruel and thoughtless tourists who at that time traveled on the boats. An old record says that practically every person aboard carried a gun of some sort, many of them having two or three. As the steamer ploughed along, these wretches shot at everything, although the boat was never stopped to collect the spoils. They were left to drift on the water if shot outright, food for fish or alligator. Wounded birds were doomed to suffer until death released them or they fell prey to something else.

The greed that almost wiped out the beautiful American egret cannot be forgotten or forgiven either. The delicate, lovely, lacy plumes of this bird, only worn with the nuptial plumage, were much sought after by the millinery trade. The vandals who shot these birds to get the few feathers cared nothing at all about the tragedies and torments they caused. Most of these herons would be nesting in large rookeries. The men would go in, shoot every bird they could, and leave the young to perish slowly of hunger. They shot roseate spoonbills also, as well as gulls and terns, for often a whole bird would "adorn" a hat. Other birds, such as cormorants and anhingas, while their feathers were not valued as highly, were killed through sheer wantonness.

Women were told that most of the feathers, especially egret plumes, were picked up under trees, that it was not necessary to kill the birds. Of course this falsehood was easily disproved and when pictures of the pitiful, starved skeletons of young birds left to die in agony or the piles of dead or wounded birds in a rookery were shown, the sales fell off.

By 1900 most of the American egrets were wiped out and spoonbills were becoming very rare. Fortunately, patient and steady work by many lovers of wild life brought about the passing of a bill making it illegal to buy or sell the plumage of birds. The murder of one of the game wardens in Florida helped bring this about; the publicity roused people to a realization of what was being carried on and the need for a bill of this type.

With the ban on the use of feathers on hats, the rookeries became safer and, once again, the flocks of birds are increasing wherever they have space to nest, usually on small islands, built up of shells and other material on which mangroves have started. The Causeway crossing from Tampa to Clearwater was, for years, a wonderful nesting site for skimmers, terns, and other birds. Recently it was turned into a recreation center for people who liked to fish, to cook out-of-door meals, and to swim. The birds, disturbed by the constant traffic and, in many cases, by having their nests run over by a car, have had to find other sites. Recently we were delighted to learn that the new fill-in on the Bellair Causeway had been taken over by least terns and black skimmers. At once signs were put up prohibiting parking or walking anywhere along the beaches there, because people had been killing so many birds, young and old alike, by driving over the nests. Now the place has been proclaimed a sanctuary, through the excellent work of the bird clubs of Tampa, St. Petersburg, and Clearwater so more birds will be safe.

There are a number of small islets and cays off the coast which have not been developed or taken over yet, and on these herons, pelicans, ibis, and other birds may find nesting facilities. Some illegal traffic in eggs and feathers still goes on but guardians are constantly on the watch to make sure the nesting colonies are not disturbed. Equipped with fast boats, they can overtake the intruders and make sure they are punished.

There are only a few places in Florida where we find any elevations and these are mostly in the central portion. Almost all of the peninsula is less than three hundred and fifty feet above sea level. Nevertheless there is quite a diversity in the areas. Just as long as there is water near by, where plenty of fish may be obtained, and tall, strong trees for nesting sites, the bald eagle finds most of these satisfactory. Their preferred homesites are along the west coast where, until a few years ago, there were many tall pines and cypresses sturdy enough to bear the weight of their huge eyries.

Moreover, until recently there were many places along the coast where few, if any, people lived or ventured in except to fish. Here the bald eagle reigned supreme, living well on food from the sea. We have seen twenty-three fresh fish, mostly cats or mullet, in one nest. They also find plenty of raccoons, swamp rabbits, and other animals in these regions.

When the retreating tide leaves a number of fish high and dry, the eagles gather for a feast. When fish stay in deep water, the King of the Air takes tribute from osprey or screaming gull, although he can, and does, go right into the water after his prey whenever it becomes necessary.

The boom in building, begun during the war and accelerating since, has changed this picture. Most of the large trees have been cut down; out of the way spots, especially near the water, have been cleared of brush or, if low, filled in with sand pumped from the bays so that cottages, motels, and restaurants could be built on them. It is hard to find any areas there now that have not been taken over bodily by the tourist or realtor.

Undoubtedly the bald eagle, once abundant throughout North America from about middle Hudson Bay in the far north to as far south as, or even into, Mexico, has gradually retreated before advancing settlement to a last stand in Alaska in the north and Florida in the south.

In Alaska the bounty on the eagle is rapidly cutting down their numbers, while in Florida, though they are protected, they will soon have few nesting sites left except in cypress swamps unless we act quickly to set aside more areas like Everglades National Park, where they will be secure from intrusion and have trees large enough to build in.

When people claim that there are so many bald eagles left in Alaska that it would be impossible to wipe them out, we should remind them again of Gilbert White's note in 1772 when he said, "Belon, two hundred years ago gives a curious account of the incredible armies of hawks and kites which he saw in the spring-time traversing the Thracian Bosphorus from Asia to Europe. Besides the above mentioned he remarks that the procession is swelled by whole troops of eagles and vultures."

Yet years ago in the British Isles they lost their last sea eagle—the brown-headed type of our bird—and in a small country in northwestern Europe there is a monument on the spot where the last pair of sea eagles nested. It happened there, it can happen here, just as we lost our passenger pigeons which, not too long ago, flew in flocks that darkened the sky—and now not one remains.

Every state should glory in the presence of the majestic symbol of their nation and indeed a great many do. In Florida the protection of the local eagles is a matter of pride. They realize their attraction value. Anyone molesting them is in for serious trouble. Charlie has had policemen come speeding down the road after him when he went up into a tree to begin banding. Now he lets the chief of police in a district know before he starts tagging there. Often they will come out to watch him at work. He likes to know that people are anxious enough about their eagles to report him, and will take time to get their names from the chief and hunt them up so he can tell them how pleased he is to know that they are looking out for the fine birds and ready to prevent anyone taking eggs or young. He explains just what he is doing and why, and often suggests that they come to see him at work if he plans to do any more nests in that vicinity.

In return, once he has calmed their fears for their protégés, he obtains a great deal of valuable information. They keep track of the arrival of the adults in the fall and the departure of the young and parents in the spring. Too, they often let him know if a nest is active—that is, if the pair are using it—when it is too far away for him to check often.

There are said to be eight eagle's nests in New Jersey, but if that is so we do not know where they are nor can any of our bird-loving friends locate them. The estimate for Maryland, Washington, and Virginia is given as one hundred and twenty-five nests. We fear the figure may be lower. This spring [1951] when Charlie asked Mr. Bryant Tyrell, who has made a most comprehensive study of the eyries in the vicinity of Washington, how many active nests he had, he very sadly replied: "Not one." This may have been due to the very bad storm of last fall—of which we shall say more later.

Maine reputedly has twenty nests, and we were told that two at least were being used in 1951. The Lake Erie region is credited with eight, while Pennsylvania has three. With those of eastern Canada and a few on the Santa Barbara Islands off the coast of California, this just about makes our total except for the Alaskan nests.

Near Baltimore we saw a splendid structure two years ago. It has been in use for a great many years. We were told of another but, though we tramped many miles, we were unable to find it.

Osprey's nests are sometimes taken to be those of the eagle but, as a rule, the osprey builds right on the top of a dead tree or stub. An eagle will sometimes do this, but not often.

Thousands of the people who revere the bald eagle as the emblem of their country have never seen one. Many will travel miles to glimpse one or if promised a sight of a nest. Charlie says he himself had never seen one until he was twenty-one. There are a number of nests in eastern Canada, and British Columbia and the Mackenzie Valley have some, but as so much of this territory is still wilderness it is impossible to say just how many there are.

Out on the prairies of Manitoba bald eagles are rare. There are no large trees in which they can build their eyries. At one of the early air meets in Winnipeg, when about five planes were present, Charlie went out to see these ships in the air but remained to watch an eagle which had followed the bigger birds in and was flying about above them, looking them over.

The next year he went out again, not to see the airplanes but to look for eagles, and sure enough there were two of them in sight.

The hammocks, so often referred to in Florida, consist of a dense growth of trees, other than pine, in comparatively dry soil. This is not wet enough to be called a swamp but is in regions where open pine prevail. Where the soil is wet enough to make it swampy the spot will be called a "low hammock." The vegetation in hammocks is a very dense growth of oaks, holly, red bay, cypress, magnolias, and other trees, as well as the ubiquitous cabbage palmetto. Such a thick growth is not attractive to big birds like the eagles. They need space around them with clear places for flying to and fro.

They prefer to be near water and do not like to have another pair nesting too near them. One pair often has two or three nests which are used in different years.

The climate of Florida seems especially suitable for bald

eagles. Nesting as they do from late November to late April, there is little chance of eggs or small young being chilled. At this time also, the sun is not hot enough to be dangerous to the young birds, although they must be shaded on a hot, sunny day. Food is plentiful and easily caught. When the days grow really warm, the birds are free from home cares, ready to travel north for the summer. Certainly it seems an ideal spot for them.

CHAPTER THREE

Finding Nests

No SOONER had the Broley family been settled in Tampa, Florida, a city chosen because of the excellent school in which daughter Jeanne was soon enrolled, than the search for nests began.

Even on the trip down, large trees had been scanned and two nests had been located, one up on Butler's Island and the other near Cross Creek, the home of Margery Kinnan Rawlings. Both were pretty far from Tampa, so daily trips were taken to near-by districts to try and discover some that were closer if possible.

To questions about nests the reply usually was, "Oh, there aren't any eagles here. You look for them up north, around mountains. Lots of buzzards,"—the common name for the vulture—"but no eagles."

We learned later that even people who had a pair of eagles nesting near them would not tell about it for fear someone might shoot them or take the eggs.

A few told us about a nest over near Bel Air in a well publicized garden, but at first Charlie was afraid he had come to the wrong part of Florida to carry out his promise.

Then he was driving slowly along, just south of Tampa, when he noticed a large, dark mass in a tree which was almost hidden by other foliage. He had to make several attempts before he found a trail leading towards it but his glimpses, as it came into view, made him more convinced. At last, after bumping through palmettos, over clusters of shrubs and small trees, he got close enough to see that it really was a huge nest.

Parking the car on the side of a narrow trail and sending up a fervent prayer that no other vehicle would come along for awhile, he made his way through fronds, scrub, and vines with horrible thorns towards his goal. Through his binoculars he studied it. Then he caught sight of a splendid white-headed eagle perched on a dead tree near by.

This was it! He had a nest so close to town that he could visit it often. Were the birds using it?

Back in the car he sat, field glasses held to his eyes, and watched the nest. At long last he was rewarded by the sight of another eagle flying in with a big stick. He watched as she fitted this into the nest, first here, then there. He counted ten times that she moved it about before she had it placed to suit her. He could tell that much of the top of the big structure was new. They were repairing it; they had most of it ready, it seemed, so they should use it all right.

For weeks he spent some time every day watching building operations. He decided to fashion a hide or blind near by from which he could observe without alarming the birds. Poultry fencing, some canvas, and a lot of palmetto leaves made an excellent shelter which did not seem to bother the big birds at all.

He was able to tell when incubation began, for now the white head could be seen for lengthy periods in one spot, showing just above the edge. When she was disturbed she would fly off, scolding—but not going far away—and would settle back on her eggs as soon as possible afterwards. It would be some time before the young would hatch. Now was the time to seek more nests.

Driving slowly about, he located a few more eyries within several miles of the first one. All were in pines and near the coast. In every case they were at least a mile apart. He went north and found nests near Tarpon Springs, Newport Richey, and Dunedin. Straight west, around Clearwater he discovered several others. About forty miles from Tampa he found some in tall cypresses and in St. Petersburg, among other sites, he found one on a golf course, one in the grounds of a veterans' hospital, and the giant nest—the largest, he believes, on the North American continent—right in a fashionable suburb.

Known to have been in use for upwards of forty years, this structure twists about the tree slightly as it rises for a distance of almost twenty feet. It is slightly over eight feet in width, and no doubt the sticks and other material it contains would weigh about a ton. A super nest, it is one of two in Florida where Charlie may count on finding three young.

He traveled down past Sarasota, Bradenton, and on to Fort Myers. On a large game preserve near Placida he was able to locate several nests, some with the eagle incubating, others where the bird made such an ado that he thought there might be small young; certainly there was something they valued. Now he knew that there would be some young eaglets to be banded in Florida.

A few of the nests were right in towns. One was directly behind a high school. From one he could have tossed stones to hit four houses. The adult birds paid little attention to these human neighbors.

He had been lucky enough to hit upon the very centre of the eagle region for his location. He had found nests. Soon there would be young: Now to find a boy to climb the trees and put on the bands!

CHAPTER FOUR

Observations in the Blind

HIS TRIPS to the blind at his first nest continued, even though he was warned about sitting in it. "Rattlesnakes like to hole up in a place like that," he was told. "Coral snakes and moccasins are thick around there. Better be careful."

At first he carried a stout stick to use if any reptiles came around. Then he contented himself with making plenty of noise going in and coming out. Sometimes a harmless snake would be twined about in the vines but, although he saw several and killed a few on his way in, no rattlers actually came into the blind. Mosquitoes and other insects pestered him; he found the heat enervating; but the eagles held his interest.

He discovered that both birds shared in the task of sitting on the eggs and that some fresh material, a lot of it Spanish moss, went into the nest every day.

He was amused on one occasion when he saw the male, who had been off on a fishing trip, presumably, fly in and settle on his favorite perch, a dead stump near by. At once the incubating female screamed furiously as if to tell him he had better take over and be quick about it. Father wasn't long getting there and settling on the eggs when she vacated.

Charlie says he seldom hears an eagle scream except in cases like this. When disturbed, they fly about whistling a sharp "Kac, Kac, Kac," but the real scream is reserved for special occasions. As it is begun, the bird begins to elevate its head and at the peak of the call the white head is resting almost on the dark back. It is most impressive.

On another occasion the male was perched, quietly sunning himself, while the female did a repair job on the home. The querulous "talking" she was doing must have been a scolding for his neglect of her. At any rate, after some staccato cluckings, he gave a scream, flew off, and returned in a few minutes with some moss which he carried up to the nest and then, as if he had finished his day's work, grunted a little and went back to sunning himself.

Broley tethered a chicken to a tree near the nest one day and retired to his blind to watch proceedings. Nothing happened! The birds paid no attention to the hen which scratched about, not at all intimidated by the presence of these supposed enemies.

For three days the fowl was left there, always with food and water near by. The eagles did not bother it at all. Finally Charlie took it away, deciding he might as well eat it, if the eagles wouldn't.

He was in the blind the day the first egg hatched. He knew it was so by the way the female watched from the side of the nest, head cocked, first this side, then that, as she gazed downwards. Both parents stood at the edge watching from time to time, and it was amusing to notice the air of pride they wore.

Thirty-five days had elapsed since the first egg was laid. There might be several days between the two, so she still had to remain on the nest. Of course, while the eaglets are small one parent is on guard all the time, anyway, for the tiny creatures must be shielded from the sun, kept warm in chilly weather, or protected from any danger. The mate brings in food, which is torn up and fed to the babies. Leftovers are finished up by the adults or left in the nest for another feeding.

When birds are brought in, it is amazing to see how the mother plucks them. The feathers go off in a perfect stream. An eagle's beak is most powerful, and it is surprising to watch one of these birds tear up a sizeable fish. Usually a large object is held down with one foot while dismembering is done.

Just before the eggs hatch, the female builds a little railing around the eggs in the centre of the nest, making a shallow, saucer-like depression about twenty inches in diameter. This is soon broken down after the babies emerge and begin to move about a little.

In Florida, eagles often cover the eggs with lining material in the period before incubation is begun, during absences from the nest, and also during short intervals when they leave the eyrie afterwards. More lining is used in Florida nests than in those of the north, owing perhaps to the abundance of Spanish moss which hangs everywhere in tremendous masses.

During all stages of incubation, brooding, and even

when the young are a good size, the adults continue to bring in liberal quantities of this moss, a great help in keeping the nests clean and sanitary.

Many people think of these nests as being deep and hollow, but they are not. Each year they are built up and are only slightly concave on top. When the adult is brooding, the white head may be seen, but it is higher than it was during the time of incubation, and the wings are elevated a bit. Charlie can tell at once by her position whether she has eggs or small young.

Bones, skin, and unedible matter are tossed from the nest or covered up. Even addled eggs may sometimes be located deep in the lining. One was buried under about one foot of moss, grass, fine roots, and twigs, showing how much material is brought in during incubation, for it was a new nest that season.

CHAPTER FIVE

A Boy to Climb?

WHILE LOCATING nests, observing from the blind, and getting ready for banding, Charlie had not forgotten about trying to find a boy to do the climbing.

He was returning from a locating trip when he overtook two lads of about fifteen or so trudging home along the highway. He offered them a lift, which they gladly accepted. His questioning soon brought to light the fact that they were quite interested in nature and the denizens of the wild. They had discovered an owl's nest and were, they said, trying to find some way to get up to it so that they could take one of the young for a pet.

The great horned owl is really a menace to a lot of our birds and is not protected by law. Broley said he'd go with them and see the nest. Probably he could show them how to get up to it.

He had studied the trees and decided that since, almost without exception, the first limb was some forty feet at least from the ground, a ladder of sorts was the only practical method of getting up to the eyrie. He had decided against climbing-irons such as telephone and linemen wear since, with them on, it would be impossible to get up onto a nest. Besides a great many of the trees there are dead and the irons will not go firmly in the punk wood inside the outer bark.

Many of the nests are built out, so that going up is like rising under an opened umbrella. He has to use an extra ladder with these and he makes sure this nest ladder, as he calls it, while light, is very strong, for it is used only up in high spots and must be put in place while he is precariously perched among the branches.

It was going to be quite a walk in to get to some of the nests so he did not want too heavy a ladder, but he had to have something he could rely upon. Ropes with wooden rungs seemed the answer so he had built a ladder forty-five feet long. To get this up into the tree he had worked out a not too difficult method. He purchased some lead weights, the type called "sinkers" by fishermen, about two to four ounces each. One of these was attached to a fine, strong cord. Spreading a large piece of canvas out on the ground below the tree containing the nest, he'd run this string back and forth across it so that it would reel out freely. Then, winding up as a baseball pitcher does, he tossed the weight up and over the first limb.

Fortunately he has a very keen eye and good muscular co-ordination, so usually it did not take too long to make this first connection. Sometimes, though, the cord would snarl or tangle on the rough bark of the tree, or catch in other branches so that the weight would not come down.

One very windy day, he tried so often and had the line catch on the bark or blow away that he "threw his arm out," as they say. After that he took a large kitchen spoon, bent it to make a deeper hollow to hold the weight, fastened it securely to the end of a light rod and used this to toss the sinker over.

His skill at lacrosse, which he had starred in as a boy, was a great help in putting the weight over, so he found this method very effective. Recently he discovered a better way. This he calls his "sure fire" method of getting a first connection.

Two years ago Otto Pelham of Tampa gave him a fisherman's casting spool; on this he winds his twenty-five-pound test nylon cord. This proved to be a wonderful idea and he no longer has to loop his line back and forth across the canvas for, from the reel, it runs easily, never tangling, never snarling. He says it is remarkable how much time he saves just with this alone and suggests that, had he owned it when he began his banding, he might have had a larger list of eagles. As he never passed up a nest, no matter how high the first limb was from the ground, it is hard to know how that could have been possible.

He uses a catapult or "sling shot" now to shoot the weight up and usually puts it through the crotch he has chosen on the very first shot. When the cord comes down to him, he ties a clothes line to it and pulls this over. Next a heavy rope is attached to this and, last of all, the ladder is fastened to the rope and hauled into place. He secures his rope around the trunk of the tree and is now ready to go up.

The owl's nest was some fifty-five feet up in a tall pine. He thought he should make the first climb himself to test his equipment and work out the best method for climbing. Accordingly he went to the nest without taking the boys along. Climbing it sideways, a foot on each side of the ladder, was the best way. It did not swing him out so far and, although it still sways dizzily, he feels he has more control of it. He hangs on only to the rope nearest to him and goes up so lightly and quickly that it looks very easy until one tries it.

There were some fairly good branches above the ladder and he took a rope up to aid in the long stretches between. He had little difficulty reaching the nest. There were two eggs in it, and while he was admiring them the mother owl returned. Owls fly silently, unlike eagles whose flight feathers make a swishing sound, so he did not hear her approach. Suddenly he was struck a prodigious blow on the back, almost knocking him from the tree. Her talons tore his shirt and drew blood from his skin.

Fortunately he had an arm around the tree, so he tightened his hold. She came in again, raking him several times. He took a picture of nest and eggs and then retreated down the tree, promising himself he'd return when the young had hatched. The owl flew about the tree as he descended and while he was unfastening the rope and hauling down his ladder but made no further attempt to strike him.

On the next trip to this nest he took the two boys along as they were very anxious to see the baby owls. They wanted to climb up as soon as the ladder was in place but Charlie thought he had better try to scare the owl away. He knew she would be much more aggressive, now that the young had hatched.

As soon as he was level with the nest, he picked up a fair sized stick from it, planning to ward her off when she came at him. She attacked him from the front this time, and, as he moved the branch out to deflect her, struck so furiously that he got stick and owl right in the face. He felt the blood pouring from gashes just near his eyes and hoped that she had not damaged them. In spite of his cuts, and half blinded by blood, he took a couple of pictures of the baby owls while warding her off.   793411

The red-headed lad wanted to go up and, when he was warned to be careful, said, "I'll kill her if she bothers me. I'll grab a stick and whack her—"

"Don't hurt her at all," Broley said. "She's only defending her babies. Ward her off so she can't injure you, but don't hit her too hard."

The boy went up the tree, muttering angrily and paying no attention to what Charlie said about the way to climb the ladder. Fortunately the owl did not molest him as the two on the ground were making so much noise that she did not know which intruder to go after. The lad had been told not to touch the young birds until they were older so, urged from the ground, he reluctantly left them there and started his descent. Again he paid no attention to advice about branches or ropes. Using the face of the ladder he was swung into the trunk of the tree and found it very difficult to get proper handholds.

On the homeward drive he repeated that he'd kill any old bird that bothered him. He said he was going to take an owlet for a pet, maybe both of them. He added that he thought he might take a young eagle also.

Charlie did not say very much. He had made his decision. He would do his own climbing; then he wouldn't have to worry about any injuries to a boy; he would know that the band was properly closed, edges firmly and evenly brought together; and, best of all, he'd be sure no harm would come to the eaglets.

CHAPTER SIX

First Banding

THE YOUNG birds in the nest where he had made his blind were not yet big enough to band when he set out on an exploratory trip down south of Sarasota. One of the first nests he discovered contained two large young, almost, he thought, ready to leave. He decided to band them at once, for they might go off very soon and he didn't want to miss any of his birds.

Getting his ladder up and all his equipment ready, he stuffed bands and pliers in his pockets and started up the tree. He could see that one young fellow was teetering near the edge of the nest and was afraid it might jump off.

Sure enough, just as he reached the top of the eyrie, master eaglet flopped out and planed off, landing in some palmettos about four hundred feet away. He marked the spot as well as he could, for he could see that the bird was not able to fly and so would have to be put back in the nest again.

The one in the eyrie fought him fiercely, tearing at his hands while he put on the aluminum bracelet marked "Notify Fish and Wild Life Service, Washington" and the number, making sure that it was smooth so that no ends would catch on vines, twigs, or anything that might imprison the creature. Then he went down after the first one.

The adults will not feed a bird on the ground, so he wanted to make sure this youngster was back up where he would be fed and cared for.

It took some time to locate him and more to capture him, for he could move swiftly and his talons were quite formidable. At last, though, he had the bird safely banded. He fastened him up in a piece of canvas despite a struggle and carried him back to the tree, then up to the nest where he seemed content to remain.

Charlie has since had to do this some fifty or more times, although he does try to tag them before they get big enough to want to start off. In the 1951 season in Ontario Charlie had to catch a big young one when he returned to the nest with some friends who wanted to get pictures. The bird was only ten weeks old, so Charlie did not expect it to be able to fly, but it could do so. The mate, an older bird, went away off but this chap dropped down after about two miles. Charlie thought it would be safe enough on the ground but preferred to put it back. He said it was a very heavy eaglet—much heavier than one of the same age would have been in Florida, and he and the two men with him were sure it would go well over fifteen pounds. Getting it up wasn't so easy, but he did it and the bird stayed on the nest after his journey up.

Charlie says when there are two well-grown birds in a nest, the young male, being the more nervous of the two, will jump off while the young female fights him. Now when he goes up to a nest where the birds are pretty well grown, he carries a stick with a hook on the end of it such as poultry raisers use. He gets this hook around the foot of the timid bird and pulls it over to him, holding it there while he bands the pugnacious female.

A great many people ask to be allowed to go with him to watch the banding, some to take pictures, a few to try climbing the swaying, swinging ladder, but most of them just to get a vicarious thrill from seeing the fine eagles, the big nest, and the sight of Charlie pulling himself up monkey-like from limb to limb.

Up in Canada, a couple of officials on the staff of the Bank of Montreal in Athens, Ontario, told Charlie about a nest on near-by Charleston Lake and suggested accompanying him to watch banding operations. They couldn't get away from the office until late afternoon and he did not like leaving it so late, although up there in June, daylight lingers.

The young birds were quite large, they said, so it would not do to wait too long and, as this seemed their only time available, he decided to go the following day, a Friday.

"How high is the first limb from the ground?" he asked.

He noticed they seemed to consult each other with eyes and eyebrows and then one said, "Oh, just about twenty-five feet."

They told him they'd take him up the lake in a boat with an outboard engine, that it really wasn't too far and shouldn't take so very long.

Friday afternoon, after some delays, they started off. Unfortunately, something went wrong with their engine and they had to row for some two and a half miles against a stiff wind, so they did not reach the spot until after seven in the evening.

At the tree Charlie discovered that the first limb was not twenty-five but sixty-five feet from the ground. The eaglets were almost ready to fly and would very likely jump out when he neared the top and have to be put back again.

The young men were so disappointed when he said he thought it was too late to begin that night that he relented and against his better judgement decided to go ahead anyway.

The wind kept blowing his line away so that he had a hard time making his first connection; he was then using the first method of throwing the weight over, but finally he was successful and soon got his ladder in place. When he was level with the nest, he tried to get his hook around the talon of the timid bird to keep it from lurching out of the nest, but it backed so far away to evade him that it toppled from the eyrie, landing in the top of a birch tree and getting all tangled up in a vine which ran through the upper branches. He banded the scrappy eaglet, getting torn up a bit in the process, and descended, ready to take down his ladder, put it up to the birch tree, climb up and get the youngster and bring him down.

But it was now nine-thirty, too dark to risk taking him back to the nest. Charlie has never left a bird on the ground if it cannot fly so he had to put this one where it would be safe until he could return. He took it up to the first limb, intending to return first thing next morning by himself and get it back to its cradle.

Meanwhile the family had been expecting him home around eight o'clock and could not imagine where he could be. He says he had to do some tall explaining when he did arrive after twelve.

When he awakened early the next morning it was raining very hard. He doesn't climb when it is wet for ropes and ladders are too slippery and so are the branches, making it very dangerous.

The following day he had an engagement with the National Film Board, some distance away, so it was not until Monday that he was able to get back there. He took his own outboard engine and got to the tree in good time. A wind storm had passed through on Sunday evening and his young eagle had been blown down onto the ground. It was doubtful if it had been fed in all that time, yet it seemed full of fight, so much so that Charlie had some difficulty banding it.

He had brought along an empty orange crate in which to put the eaglet while he hauled it up to the nest, so he got it in, fastening it well and, climbing up, soon drew the crate up.

When he released the bird it scrambled over to join its sister, who had gone over to a stub on the side of the nest to get away, knocked her off and, losing its balance, tumbled out of the tree again.

Again Charlie had to go down and hunt out the hiding places. They had floundered over to a little island near by and were well hidden under some bushes. He managed to catch them, however, one at a time, and, carrying them over to the crate, got them both in. He said he was sure the box had never been so full of oranges as it was of eagles.

When he pulled the young birds up, he was careful to place them right in the center of the nest and this time they stayed put.

All in all, banding these two birds had required about ten hours of his time. It is fortunate that not all his eaglets cause him so much trouble.

Getting up and onto some of his nests, he discovered, would require an additional ladder about fifteen feet or more in length. He built this so that, though light in weight, it would be sound and strong. He did not relish the idea of rotating around, some seventy feet up in the air, on a ladder that might go to pieces.

Some of the nests are so high up, with few or no branches on the tree, that it is necessary to make the first connection right over the top of the nest. This means ninety feet or more of ladders. He carries extra ones when he visits such trees and ties several together. Sometimes he draws his first ladder up into the tree after he has reached the first branch. This means that he cannot anchor it around the tree at the bottom but must leave it free. Needless to add, he swings about wildly at times.

Ropes and ladders need to be tested often, for they will wear out. During the war, because of priorities on good rope, it was hard for him to buy what he needed, so he spliced, bound, and waxed what he had to make it do. Once, in 1942, when his longest ladder was showing evidence of wear, he asked Fred Lane, manager of a Tampa hardware store, if there was any possibility of obtaining new rope. Mr. Lane replied that, while he would hate to see Charlie fall and break his neck, the O.P.A. did not appear to mention eagle banders in their list of those with priority. He was sorry, but he could not help him at all.

Charlie was just turning, disappointed, to leave the shop when his friend snapped his fingers suddenly and said, "Just a minute! Come to think of it we have an unusual coil of Italian rope that I don't believe the O.P.A. ever heard of. At any rate it isn't mentioned on the list. Let's take a look at it."

He found the coil, called Italian Hemp Bolt Rope. It was used for rigging on high masts. While it was expensive, it was very strong and Charlie was assured that it would last for years. Today, after nine years of strenuous use it is still giving splendid service.

Where there are few branches, Charlie often uses an extra rope with a weight on one end, slinging it over a higher branch and pulling himself up on it.

How he can maintain his balance while tossing this up is always amazing. It is possibly the most nerve-racking part of his climb for onlookers; certainly it is for me.

Perhaps the most difficult climb for my husband was the one tree I climbed. I was to give some radio talks, and it had been suggested that, to add realism, I say: "We climb" and "We band." This I certainly could not do unless I had at least one tree and one bird to my credit, so I asked Charlie to find a very low nest in an easy tree. I don't suffer from acrophobia but, nevertheless, I didn't think I could clamber from limb to limb as he does. He assured me he had an almost foolproof tree not too far away and agreed to help me get up.

We drove out early one morning, equipped with ladders, ropes, and other impedimenta. After parking the car on a side road, we walked across the wet sand to the big pine in which I could see the large nest, about fifty-five feet from the ground.

Charlie got the ladder up and into place, ascended to test everything and to show me how, and on which branches to go up after reaching the top of the ladder. Then he came down to give last directions. He suggested putting a rope on me; one of our friends had mentioned a bosun's chair as the best method, but I wasn't that clumsy, I hoped.

I started up and he directed me, standing anxiously below, ready to take the pictures I wanted. I am no climber but I did manage with all his help. Coming down was rather hazardous, but I made it and soon was safe at the bottom again. Charlie was streaming with nervous perspiration but he smiled gaily and said, "That wasn't bad now, was it?"

I tried to make my "No, indeed" as convincing as possible but did not add that it was quite enough for me. I've climbed one tree, I've banded one bird, and that's the extent of it. He can do the rest. I did not tell him that I could see how much worry it had caused him, nor that I realized that when he went up to the nest again he carefully worked at the band I had put on the baby eagle—it was just large enough to tag, a bare three weeks old—to make sure it was smooth-fitting. These bands are pretty stiff, and strong fingers are required, as well as pliers, to make sure they do meet snugly.

Jeanne has been up several times but she, naturally, is much more agile than I. Also she has her father's quickness of mind and marvellous co-ordination so I do not worry too much when she goes climbing with him.

There is one nest, however, where I am always delighted to hear that there are no young in the spring. This, a red-tailed hawk's, is up in Canada on a ledge at the side of quite a high hill boasting the rather strange name of Rock Dundar, and it is about forty feet from the top.

From this ledge there is a straight drop, one hundred and fifty feet to the sparkling blue water below. The walk to the top, while gradual, is long and usually pretty tiresome, especially if we are burdened with ropes and ladders. We stop to study warblers, to recognize flowers, or to study ferns as we go along. At the top, after Charlie has crawled to the edge to see what is in the nest, he gets his ladder down, instead of up, anchoring it to a huge stone. They laugh at me because I generally stand on the ladder to hold it also.

I breathe a sigh of thankfulness when they climb back to the top, grinning at my worried face, to report that the bands are on and I can relax for another year.

CHAPTER SEVEN

Plumages, Appearance, and Behavior

THOUGH THE magnificent bald or white-headed eagle, *Haliaeetus Leucocephalus*, is their emblem, there are thousands of people in the United States who have never seen one. At one time this large bird with the pure white tail and head was quite common on the continent of North America. As the land was settled it was driven from area after area until at the present time the bald eagle population is concentrated in Florida and Alaska, the two extremes.

The Alaskan bird, *Haliaeetus Alascanus*, is somewhat the larger of the subspecies and its range extends southward possibly to just north of South Carolina. The Florida eagle, *Haliaeetus Leucocephalus Leucocephalus*, while somewhat smaller in size, builds a larger nest and, according to Broley, the young are very much fiercer and harder to handle.

The appearance of this bird makes it unmistakable. It is larger than any of the hawks or vultures and the pure white head and tail identify it from the Golden eagle. The body is fuscous and the primary feathers are blackish brown. The great wingspread is from seventy-two to ninety inches across.

The flight of an eagle is most distinctive, very heavy looking as it goes along with slow flaps, but on a windy day when it soars in great circles at an immense height it is a marvel of grace and beauty. Watchers are often lucky enough to see it dive, with half-closed wings, or dart with lightning speed after something it sees.

The young, or immature, are dark and look much like a very large hawk. Perhaps some are shot as hawks in their first years of life. This is the bird Audubon identified as the Washington eagle, thinking it was a separate species.

When first hatched the young eaglet is covered with long, thick, silky down which is longest on the head. It is a smoky grey on the back, paler grey on the head and underparts and nearly white on the throat. In about three weeks this lightish down is pushed out to be replaced by short, thick down almost like lamb's wool, of a very dark, greyish color. Soon the plumage begins to appear on body and wings with scattered, brownish black feathers showing on the scapulars and the back and sides of the breast when the bird is about five or six weeks old. Much time is spent by the youngster preening these new feathers and getting rid of whatever grey down is left. This gives it a somewhat ragged appearance for awhile, and bits of grey down fly off in the breeze, or land in trees and bushes about.

The wing quills begin to break through their sheaths when the bird reaches its fifth or sixth week and by the time it is seven or eight weeks old, the eaglet is fairly well feathered and only a little down shows.

The flight feathers even at this age are half-grown, giving an odd, drooping appearance to the wings; the young bird seems to have difficulty keeping them up or out.

In its fresh, juvenal plumage the bird is uniformly dark, appearing almost black in some lights and brown in others. Very often, though, there is a sprinkling of greyish white in the tail, foretelling the future pure white. This costume is worn for the first year with little change except that of fading and wear.

Both adult eagles and young have one complete moult a year but this is very gradual, being prolonged through spring, summer, and fall. The flight feathers are usually moulting during July, August, and September.

The second year the plumage of the young becomes paler with some white mixed in. The following year there are many more white feathers in the plumage, especially in the tail, and most of the feathers of the head are tipped with tan. The fourth year, tail and head show quite a bit of white and the body is much darker, almost like that of an adult. In its fifth year, the bird acquires the white head and tail and is now ready to mate and rear its family.

The voice of the eagle sounds much like the grunting of a pig as it flies low over the nest when intruders are about. When alarmed, the "Kac, Kac" note is given, high pitched and staccato. The scream of an eagle is seldom heard but it is well worth watching the screaming performance, for the head is elevated and pulled back until at the peak of the cry it is practically touching the back, with the great yellow bill pointing straight up. The call of the female is harsher and more broken, and she can usually be picked out by this.

Young eagles have a plaintive, squealing note that sounds

somewhat like "pee, pee-e," especially when they are hungry and the parents have been away a long time. The note when the parents are seen coming back to the nest is higher and much faster as they move quickly over to the side of the nest where they expect them to come in, anxious to grab the food first.

While the young bald eagle might be confused with a golden eagle, it lacks the golden hackles on neck and head. Besides this, the young golden has more white in the basal half of the tail than a first year bald. Older immature birds show more or less white on breast and belly which the golden does not have. The tails of immature species show quite a bit of white, but the golden has a distinct dark band. When flying, the bald eagle stretches its head and neck out much more than any other eagle or hawk except the Mexican caracara. Of course the bare tarsus of the bald will distinguish it from the feathered one of the golden in any plumage.

Eagles spend a great deal of time sitting motionless on some favorite perch, especially when not busy with household cares. In Alaska, it is possible to see many of these birds together sitting in the same or near-by trees, and no slightest movement, no unusual glint escapes their quick eyes. The eagle eye as a term for strength and swiftness of vision is no misnomer. That yellow iris, the color of the sun whose representative the bird was long thought to be, has a keenness equalled by that of few, if any other, birds. This, in the immature, is dark and doesn't fully change until near maturity. The brilliant yellow beak is not attained, either, until about that time.

During the wintertime in Florida it is possible to see a number of young eagles, two years or so in age, congregating together. Adults also may be seen in goodly numbers on cool days, when the fish seem stupid and are often left in holes on the flats when the tide recedes. Then there is plenty for all and no need to fight over food.

When chasing a large bird, such as a duck or goose, the apparently slow, heavy flight of an eagle becomes swift and dashing. It quickly overtakes its prey which, realizing the peril, flees ahead or tries to evade by swift turns to right or left. But an eagle is not to be misled. Speeding on, it sweeps beneath the unlucky quarry and, turning half over, thrusts its powerful talons into the breast of the victim. Smaller birds are then carried to the nearest sand bar or marsh, but when the prey happens to be a Canada goose or a bird of that size, victor and vanquished fall together into the water. Then the eagle tows its prey to shore or to a sand bar or rocky islet. One was seen to take a goose in this way half a mile.

The eagle, unlike the duck hawk, prefers to make a kill over water. We have watched a duck hawk harry grouse until he drove them to where he could swoop above land, whereas the eagle will turn them back to the water. It does kill above land, too, but usually only smaller birds and mammals.

Many people have thought that the bald eagle would not attack a large heron, a pelican, or a sandhill crane but in one nest near Punta Gorda in Florida, Charlie has found skeletons of Ward's herons, brown pelicans, and egrets. While the pelican looks quite large it has hollow bones and is really quite light for its size. The birds taken to these nests might have been sick, or even dead, ones, but Charlie does not believe so. He finds the long bills every season and is afraid these are, as he calls them, "bad actors."

It is believed that an eagle cannot carry more than about six pounds, certainly not as much as its own weight of ten or eleven pounds.

A young eagle at the time it leaves the nest usually weighs a pound more than its parents. This extra pound is lost once it begins to hunt for its own food.

Some writers say that the eagle, like the owl and some hawks, casts up the indigestible portions of the food it eats—that is, the bones, fur, feathers, and so forth in the form of pellets. Broley has never seen one in any nest he has examined, although he is quite familiar with the ones regurgitated by owls, especially the snowy owl. In these the hard or sharp bits are encased in the fur with the skin side out so that the throat of the bird will not be cut or scratched. There is no odor to them and insects do not seem to be attracted to them, so that it is safe to keep them around for study.

Quantities of bones will often be found in the eagle's nest or on the ground below, and he has seen the big birds plucking feathers from prey. A tame eagle which we watched for a number of years was never known to cast up pellets, either, but tore his food to pieces, leaving skin and bigger bones while he tore the meaty part into chunks and swallowed them. He generally ripped off the head of a fish first, then standing on the carcass, tore off chunks until he got at the part he desired. As with many animals, he very often ate the entrails first, as if they were the choicest portion.

When the eaglets are small it is touching to see the way the parents tear the food into small pieces and put them in their bills so tenderly. The more demanding of the babies gets the greatest amount, however, for the weaker, smaller one is always neglected for the more aggressive one. As a consequence one that is a little smaller, a trifle weak, perhaps, tends to grow weaker through lack of food, abuse from the older bird, and general neglect, while the stronger one, because it gets all the food, increases in size and strength rapidly.

Watching a small eagle being fed one day, Charlie was amused to see it grab the talon of the parent and peck at it when kept waiting for a mouthful.

A nesting eagle will not tolerate a strange one in the vicinity of the eyrie. Charlie, seated in his car on the driveway of Mrs. Josselyn Van Slyke's home, near Sarasota, on January 3rd, 1946, was watching a nest in which there were two eaglets about ten days old. A strange eagle came along just at dusk and settled in a tree, possibly to spend the night. Though it was five hundred feet from the nest, the brooding eagle rushed at it and drove it away up the river.

CHAPTER EIGHT

Food of the Bald Eagle

THE EAGLE, contrary to the belief many of us hold, is a fish eater. That is why the eyries are always found near water. In Florida, there is an abundance of such food to be had and sometimes the nests contain twenty or more fish, some quite fresh, usually of the coarser, less gamey varieties.

When the tide goes out quickly ahead of a strong wind, thousands of fish are left trapped in shallow waterholes scattered over the sand flats. Then eagles regale themselves and carry many fine large fish up to their nests.

Mullet and catfish are the species most frequently found in the nests, though one sees also eel, trout, jackfish, needlefish and other kinds. Turtles are a common food—the shells show up in most eyries.

Charlie says that only on three occasions has he found the remains of poultry in nests.

One very windy day he went to a high nest with a naturalist, Wilbur Smith. On the way in Mr. Smith said, "Do you find many signs of poultry in your nests? Do you think they really do clean up on the farmer's fowl?"

"No," Charlie answered, "I've only found feet or heads in two out of seven hundred nests to which I've climbed."

After he got up to the nest he called down to Mr. Smith, "Not so good here."

Mr. Smith asked what the trouble was and Charlie, trying to make himself heard above the noise of the wind, said, "There are two chicken heads here after all my boasting."

"Throw them down," called Mr. Smith and Charlie tossed them to the ground beneath the nest. He then banded the young birds as quickly as possible and descended for, although he does not mind how high a nest is, he dislikes rocking around up there in a strong wind, especially if the tree, as often happens, seems none too solid.

"Did you find any other chicken remains?" asked Mr. Smith as Broley came down.

"To tell you the truth," Charlie answered, "the nest was swaying around so much I did not examine it as thoroughly as usual but I did not see anything else there."

"Those were the heads of Rhode Island Reds," Mr. Smith said, "and the only man around here who raises them is Charlie Fraser. Let's go over and see what he has to say about them."

Charlie was a little dubious. He had visions of Fraser coming over and shooting his magnificent, white-headed friends, but they went over to the farm.

Crossing a little bridge over a bayou, they drove into the yard and Fraser came out. After the usual talk about the weather, the crops, and so forth Charlie asked, "Do those eagles ever bother your poultry?"

"No," Mr. Fraser replied, "that nest has been there for sixteen years and they've never bothered my chickens at all."

"How do you account for these, then?" Broley asked, holding out the two heads.

Mr. Fraser laughed. "I can explain that. You see, every Saturday I get a few birds ready for market. As I go across that little bridge there, I toss the heads into the water and the gulls rush for them. Then the eagles, just to show their power, take them from the noisy rascals and carry them off. No! The eagles didn't kill those chickens."

Charlie has found bills of herons and pelicans; feathers and other remains of cormorants, mergansers, coots, and bluebill, or scaup ducks in nests. Scientists who have examined scores of eagle stomachs assure us that the amount of predation is relatively small and much of what is eaten is carrion.

The eagle is often accused of stealing young pigs, but here again the evidence disproves the theory. Charlie did find the remains of a piglet in one nest but the man who lived near by told him he thought it was one of a recent litter which had died at birth.

A fine, banded, immature bald eagle with a wingspread of seven feet was shot by a rancher who said it was taking his pigs. Charlie went down to interrogate him.

"Did you see the bird make off with a pig?" he asked.

"Well—no. But he was flying around and the pigs acted frightened. They ran all about, squealing—"

"Have you missed any of your pigs?"

"Well—I'm not sure—haven't counted them lately but there's likely some gone."

After more questioning which elicited similar vague answers, Charlie asked, "Did you ever know positively of an eagle taking a pig?"

The rancher cleared his throat, hesitated, and finally drawled, "Perhaps not, but my grandfather said eagles took pigs."

One of the nests under observation is quite near a ranch where a great many pigs are raised. The owner says the eagles have never taken any of his pigs.

At this spot, early in April, from thirty to sixty eagles, mostly immature, gather before they start the trip north. It is quite a sight to see them chasing each other and acting like a group of youngsters at play. Sows with young are wandering about, quite unworried. We did see a black vulture bite the tail right off a piglet one day there.

Half-grown raccoons are discovered in many eyries, also opossum, skunks, rats, and rabbits. A lady in Tampa told Charlie an eagle had picked up her white cat and carried it up to a big nest that used to be near her home.

There are many ospreys or fish hawks in Florida and the eagle seems to delight in making them pay tribute to his supremacy. This bird will dive right into the water after a fish, sending the spray flying. Eagles seldom do this unless hunger overcomes their dislike of a wetting. They have been seen to go completely under, though, coming up again with their prize.

When the eagle sees an osprey with its booty, he gives a sharp scream to tell him he wants it, then takes after the bird. The fish hawk will often drop the prey at once and the eagle pounces on it before it drops to the water or land.

Occasionally the hawk tries to outdistance the eagle, but a few more raucous screams from the king of the air soon make him obey orders. Once in awhile a fish, unhurt by the first bird's talons, will be lucky enough to fall into the water. By diving immediately it foils the would-be diner.

Charlie was much amused at a story told him by Mr. A. F. Johns, who owns a large market garden near Bradenton. He employs a dozen or so Negro helpers.

One day, standing near one of his oldest hands, Mr. Johns was watching an eagle chasing an osprey. He saw the hawk release the fish it was carrying when the eagle got too close. The king failed to retrieve it, however, and the fish, a fine mullet, dropped right in front of the grizzled old farmhand. He had been working away, oblivious of this byplay in the sky. It was just noon, and the Negro, picking up this fine addition to his meal, which was still alive, by the way, looked up at Mr. Johns with a smile and said, "The Lord sure am good to His chillun."

Stories of eagles carrying off children appear in magazines or papers from time to time but, so far, not one has ever been verified. Charlie has not made any tests to discover just how much an eagle could carry. He says he is leaving that for later when he is too old to climb. He believes that about seven pounds would be the limit.

In nearly every eyrie in Florida, epiphytes, or air plants about the size of an average pineapple are to be found. Sometimes as many as fourteen of these will be ranged around the edge. Often they look as if the birds had been eating them, for the long leaves will be torn and ragged, especially at the base.

Nests in Ontario have very little food in them; apparently provisioning is a more difficult matter up there.

Broley has found snakes in some nests, though no rattlers so far. A rat snake wriggled away from the side of one just as he reached the top after a stiff climb. Near Silver Springs in Florida there was a snakepit containing many rattlers. Ned Moran, who had caught a lot of these for Ross Allen, told us that every day a number of them would be missing. There was no way they could get out of the pit and he could not imagine who or what could be taking them. He decided to watch and saw a huge eagle fly in, grab a rattler by the back of its neck with a talon, then tear at it with the beak. When it flew up with the serpent, it held it with both talons which were spread wide apart as if to prevent the snake twining around legs or wings.

Mr. E. B. Ball of Sarasota has told us of seeing many reptiles caught and killed by this intrepid bird.

Some people near Bradenton who were raising ducks missed several. They were sure the eagles from a near-by nest were making away with them. They were all set to shoot the pair but Broley suggested a tour of the nearby woods first. Not far away they discovered a nest of the great horned owl and, at the foot of the tree it was in, they found the remains of the ducklings.

"There are your culprits," Broley told them. "Don't blame the eagles."

The eagle does eat carrion when it is not too old, and no doubt some of the stories told about it taking off lambs or pigs are due to the fact that it has been seen with, or tearing at, one of these animals which had either been killed or had died and been thrown out in the wilds.

We saw a cow being eaten while still alive by black vultures one day—yet who would say they could kill such a large animal? The cow had stuck fast in a muddy ditch near Myaaka State Park and, although she thrashed around and lashed at them with head and tail, the horrible black creatures were tearing out her flesh. We hurried down the road to the rancher to get him to come and get the poor thing out or else put her out of misery—we had no means of doing either. He promised to go at once and we had to leave her there, trusting that he would keep his word and not leave her to suffer too long.

As eagles cannot carry more than their own weight, eleven or so pounds, many of the tales told about the fantastic things they have carried off are ridiculous. Nor does an eagle pull his punches when he does attack. He wouldn't be content to grab a hunk of cloth and tear it out of a child's dress as one story says an eagle did. The child would have been torn a bit, also, but we do not believe that this has ever happened.

On one occasion when he got up into a big nest, Charlie found a large mullet flopping about there. It had evidently just been brought in, and he had scared the eagle off before she could tear it up. He could see no mark on it and brought it home. I cooked it for him and he said it was excellent, but I did not try it.

At other times when he has found a number of fish in a nest he has brought some home to give to Jimmy, the fine captive eagle which lived not too far from us in Tampa for a number of years.

A boy told him one day about seeing an eagle bearing a marsh rabbit fly past him and go on up to its eyrie. There it must have released its hold for the lad said the rabbit jumped right out of the nest and down to the ground. His liberty was short-lived, however, for the eagle caught him again and bore him aloft and that time he stayed up there.

Trappers in Ontario have told us about seeing an eagle drop a rabbit in winter when flying along with it, onto the icy ground. The rabbit bounced up and the big bird caught it and went aloft again to repeat the performance. We have not seen this, but have been told about it by three different trappers.

These chaps lose a lot of their spoils to the eagle, which often takes trap as well as the catch. In one nest there were sixteen such traps and in some cases the bones of the muskrat were still in them. These were the kind having an attached chain which could be slipped down a pole to anchor them and prevent the muskrat making off with them if caught by the paw. The eagle, seeing the plump animal in the trap, picked it up; the chain ran up the pole, and the whole was carried to the nest.

In Ontario, fish are not as numerous or as easily caught as in Florida and the eagles up there eat more mammals. Woodchucks are plentiful, and a tremendous nuisance to farmers for they destroy a great deal of grain, besides digging burrows in the ground which can be a menace to man or animal. A fully grown groundhog, as the farmers call them, will give a dog a good battle, although the latter usually wins in the end.

The bald eagle makes a much speedier job of destroying it.

Recently, while driving along a country road we noticed a woodchuck running wildly towards its den. Looking up, we saw an eagle make a power dive on the frantic animal. Only a few feet from the den and safety the big bird grabbed the woodchuck with both talons, turning it over and over. Then, sinking those vicious yellow toes into the throat before the animal could regain its feet, it gave one quick rip with its powerful beak, tearing the animal wide open, and the battle was over.

CHAPTER NINE

Eagles and Owls

ONE OF the enemies of successful eagle nesting in Florida is the great horned owl. These birds are very numerous there and seem much more aggressive than those of the north.

Sometimes a pair of them will take over an eyrie while the rightful owners are absent in late summer. Charlie believes all the eagles go north during the summer months. If the owls are established when they return, it is hard for the eagles to regain their property. He doubts, indeed, if many make a serious attempt to do so.

A nest at Dunedin, Florida, was taken over by owls in 1941. The eagles visited the nest frequently and inspected the young owls but they made no effort to regain possession, nor was their new nest found that season although, when dispossessed by these birds the eagle usually builds another nest. By the time they choose a suitable site and get the nest finished it is past their regular laying time so no eggs are laid that season.

In the first year of his banding, Charlie found a nest near Tampa in which a great horned owl was incubating one of its own eggs and one of a bald eagle. Both eggs were in good condition so he made plans to watch the outcome. Unfortunately, the tree was cut down before the eggs hatched.

In January of 1946, as he approached one of the nests, an eagle rose off it and flew away. He climbed the tree anyway to see if there were small young. Just as his head came up level with the top of the nest, a great horned owl whisked off, almost hitting him in the face.

She had been sitting on a single egg, not more than three feet from where the eagle was incubating but slightly lower down. One of the eagle's eggs had been broken in the fight for the site. Heavy rains made the trails impassible later so he was not able to visit the nest again. It would have been most interesting to know if the eggs of both hatched, and how the young behaved, and so forth.

On another occasion, he noticed an eagle standing on the side of a nest, apparently watching young. He climbed up to see if these babies were old enough to band, only to discover that they were young owls. He does not believe she had hatched them out, although that could be possible.

Owls see so much better at night than eagles and Broley thinks they attack at that time. People living near an occupied eagle's nest heard a disturbance at it during the night. Owls hooted, the eagles screamed, and there was much crashing of branches. Next day they discovered that the owls had possession of the nest.

Broley has handled adult eagles in the dark and they appeared very confused. Great horned owls are formidable opponents. They are extremely strong and their talons are exceedingly sharp. They are adaptable and will at times nest on the ground.

Charlie found one at the foot of a pine tree. The eggs had been laid in the grass. One fluffy white baby had already emerged and the other egg, rounder than an eagle's, was chipped.

A case of an owl nesting in a hole in the side of an occupied bald eagle nest was reported by J. Warren Jacobs in 1908. The nest was fifteen feet high and the owl's cavity was about four feet from the bottom. This seems a case of sharing a nesting tree in a sense, rather than sharing a nest.

Owls do not bother the eagles so much in Ontario, possibly because there are not so many eagle nests. They do use hawk's nests, however, and have even been found utilizing an old crow's nest.

CHAPTER TEN

Odd Objects in Eagles' Nests

ALTHOUGH THE nest itself is a towering mass of branches and limbs, the eggs of the bald eagle are laid in a small, well-formed cuplike depression lined with Spanish moss or fine grasses in the center of the top of the great pile. This moss is very plentiful in Florida and the eagles use it to cover up dead fish, refuse, even a bad egg. Charlie found a new nest on one occasion in which there was an addled egg about forty-six inches down in the moss. He usually examines the nests pretty well to make sure on what the eagles are feeding and also because the male has a queer habit of carrying unusual objects up to the nest. Whether this is for the purpose of adding a decorative touch to the domicile, for playthings for the young, or because the bird liked the bright color, he is not sure.

Often fish plugs are found there. These, of course, would be brought in with fish. What probably happened was that the fish broke the angler's line and got away with hook and lure. Then, when it was thrashing about, trying to get rid of these, the eagle spied it and soon captured it.

On one visit Charlie found a hook, with a couple of feet

of leader trailing behind, firmly imbedded in the wing of an eaglet. He had quite a time getting it out and was glad he was able to, for the bird would have been greatly hampered with all that waving around him when he flew.

He found a chlorox bottle, empty of course, and a snap clothes-pin in one eyrie, and wondered if a laundry was contemplated or if the adults had gotten sick of the fishy smell. Another eyrie held a long white candle, broken a bit. Then he found an electric light bulb—a thousand lumen, the type used in street lighting. A radio reporter whom he had told of this over the telephone, in her broadcast said he had found light bulbs, "A thousand of them!"

Old shoes, gunny or crocus sacks, ears of corn, even a family-group photograph in a heavy frame, were discovered in nests besides, naturally, the remains of animals, fish, and reptiles which the young birds or their parents had devoured. Large shells are common up in Florida eyries, conchs turning up in almost every one. The curious, crucifix like, bony structure of the catfish is found in all the nests or on the ground at the foot of the tree.

When there was so much talk a few years ago about the "new look" for women, Broley saw an eagle flying in to its nest with a long skirt trailing behind. He wondered then if they had become style conscious also. This was not the only ladies' garment found away up in the treetops. A pair of lace-trimmed pink panties reposed coyly in a corner of one big nest. Broley was much amused when one commentator, mentioning these said—and Charlie says he misquoted him—"Broley is of the opinion that the eagle took them off a line, not off a lady."

Up in an eyrie he found a copy of the *American Weekly*, the Sunday supplement for so many papers. Oddly enough, it was opened at an article about the Doukabors in Canada and the trouble they were causing the government of that country by their nude parades. He thought it was exceedingly strange to think that he, a Canadian, should be sitting up in an eyrie in Florida with a half-grown eagle on each side of him, reading this article about far-off Canada.

Charlie went one Saturday to band the young in nests in the vicinity of Ruskin. A lad named Jimmy Busbee, who often went along to help carry ladders or other equipment when he was banding in that neighborhood lived near one of the nests to which he was climbing. When he saw Charlie he asked if he would take him into Tampa as he wanted to spend the week end with his sister who was married and living there. Charlie assured him he'd take him along and the lad went off to get cleaned up while Charlie drove on to do another nest.

After he had called for the boy, who now wore his Sunday best suit of clothing, Charlie remarked, "That nest across the flats there has me puzzled. According to my notes she has been sitting on eggs for two months. They must be bad. I really should go and take them away—."

Just then he saw a fine, big, black eaglet stand up beside her. "Well," he exclaimed, "I guess I don't know my eagles as well as I thought I did. I was sure she was incubating by the way she was sitting with just her white head showing. I'll go and band that one. It must be almost six weeks old."

When they reached the tree, Jimmy sat down a little

way off, on some dry sand, anxious to keep from soiling his suit and the bander, getting his ladder up, was soon in the big nest.

He called down to the boy, "This is a find! It's really my first 'Three egg nest' in Florida. There are two fine young and an addled egg." He banded one bird, then picking up the somewhat soiled looking egg which was imbedded in the mossy lining, looked at it more closely. It was a rubber ball!

"Here, catch this rotten egg," he called, throwing it right at the boy, who turned a quick back somersault, fearing for his good clothes, imagining them ruined with a rotten egg. He had a good laugh though, when he discovered that it was a ball.

The talon marks are quite plain on the ball and, as the male is the one which brings in the queer objects, Charlie says he played a nasty trick on his mate that time.

A splendid nest he visits each year is on the popular Pasadena Golf Course near St. Petersburg. The nesting tree is on a bend in the fairway and golfers very often send sliced balls in that direction.

The female of this pair is most aggressive and swooped at and scolded intruders so the caddies did not enjoy going in after these balls. On one occasion when the bander went in to the nest he was accompanied by two lads who picked up thirty-two golf balls on the ground near the tree. Some were in excellent condition and the boys were able to sell most of them.

CHAPTER ELEVEN

Behavior

WHEN THE southern bald eagle was chosen as the emblem of the United States it was, Broley believes, an excellent choice. This American eagle is the only one found solely on the continent of North America. The golden eagle which has been suggested as a better selection is found elsewhere as well as in this country. Benjamin Franklin, who was one of the committee appointed to suggest emblems as designs for the seal of the United States, had spoken of the turkey but that barnyard fowl, while a splendid bird with which to celebrate holidays, is not the type to be a symbol for a great nation. Possibly it was because he was ridiculed for naming this garrulous strutter in the poultry run that he called the eagle a robber and a coward. He was pleased that the first design showed the chosen emblem, the bald eagle, looking more like a turkey than it should, for he claimed that, though a turkey was silly and probably vain, it did have courage.

Audubon, quoting from Franklin, said he also considered the American eagle an arrant coward and a pirate, stealing fish from osprey instead of hunting for himself. This opinion is not shared by those who have studied the home life of our bird.

The eagle is not a coward. It is true he flies away from men with guns, but which of us would be foolhardy enough to stand still and be shot? Until the advent of men with guns the eagle had little to fear. His eyrie high up in a tree was safe from marauders. He was lord over all other birds and few animals were brave enough to bother him.

While the eaglets are small the parent stays on guard, watching over them and warning those who come too near, but he hasn't anything to use against a gun so he, wisely, flies high and expects the intruder to go off and leave the young alone.

To see these eagles as they wing back and forth over the nest, stooping at times as they squeal their "Kac, Kac, Kac" warning, no one would think of them as timorous. When cornered an eagle will fight valiantly, and woe betide anyone foolish enough to get within reach of its mighty wings and tremendously strong talons. It is not a suspicious or unfriendly bird but is ready to be amicable if left alone.

As a parent the eagle is a model. Six or more months out of each year it is busy rearing its family and giving them a start in life. Nor does it, as most birds do, leave them to their own devices once they leave the home for the first time. Long after the young are well able to fend for themselves it continues to bring food to the nest and they are free to come get it when they are hungry.

It is true the eagle does take tribute from the osprey but,

after all, he is the King and must, at times, show his authority. Nevertheless, he can, and does, catch his own fish. He often dives in, much as the fish hawk does, when from on high he sees a fish in the water and, grasping it in his powerful talons, either bears it aloft or tows it to shore.

Many a fish which has broken the line of an angler is later caught by the eagle which, seeing it moving about, trying to shake the hook loose, dives in and captures it; this is proved by the many hooks and lures found in eagle nests.

The eagle does not disdain carrion, especially if it is recently dead. In Alaska, it is a common practice of fur farmers to put out dead foxes where the eagles can find them. Then they lie in wait and when the bird comes in to feed, shoot it for the two-dollar bounty, thus making something at least out of their misfortune in losing a young fox. That they may in this selfish and sneaking way wipe out our national bird means little to them, compared with the paltry sum they receive for their duplicity.

To watch an eagle going after ducks or other waterfowl is to see a most entertaining spectacle. The sight, or sound, of an eagle sends the birds into one compact mass and they remain thus until the eagle stoops at them. Then they seem to explode from the water, feet paddling noisily and wings beating rapidly. The eagle flies off and the ducks return to the water. Again the bird dives at them and once more they rise. Usually, after one or two such stoops, one of the ducks becomes separated and the eagle, marking it, chases it until he overtakes it. He then swoops below it, thrusting his ferocious talons into the plump breast and carrying it off.

Sometimes a duck or coot, for these are caught also, eludes him for a time by diving into the water. But the eagle will keep on stooping at it each time it comes to the surface until he tires it out and is able to grab it. Eagles have been seen to go right under the water after coots, ducks, and other water-loving birds, but they do not have the oily protective coating on the feathers that the fish hawk has.

Occasionally a hunter loses his prey to the eagle when the bird swoops after and carries off a wounded bird before the nimrod can retrieve it.

One Sunday morning, the day after the opening of the shooting season in Ontario, we saw a big bird flying heavily and very low over the waters of the lake on which we have our summer home. Suddenly it went down into the water. Grabbing our binoculars from the shelf near the door, we ran out and saw that it was an adult eagle, its white head shining clearly, carrying a large, dark bird of some sort. Another bald eagle was flying near it but making no effort to take the burden.

After a few minutes' rest the eagle started up with his trophy and flew quite a little distance before going down into the water again. We could not tell what he was carrying. He managed to rise and struggle on a little further. The strong wind into which he was heading was too much for him, though, and he dropped his booty. At once the other eagle picked it up and both went on and over to a near-by rocky islet.

We got a boat and hurried over to see what his burden had been. Quite a distance away we could tell all right for feathers were floating past us in the water. The eagle was busily plucking a black duck.

We thought it must have been one that was either wounded or killed and not found by the hunter. What surprised us was that its weight—about three pounds—should have been too much for the first eagle. Perhaps it was soaked with water, which would make it heavier, and undoubtedly the eagle had flown from the Upper Lake, a long stretch for it when carrying a burden and bucking a strong wind.

Eagles are easily tamed and in the days of falconry were often used with other hawks to hunt down game. The Kirghiz and wandering tribesmen of Central Asia for centuries used relatives of our eagle to bring down meat.

This work was best accomplished in open, level country where the eagle could overtake its quarry in the open. During such a flight the usually ponderous winging of an eagle became exceedingly swift and graceful. When close to its victim the great bird would sweep beneath it to deliver the *coup de grâce*, turning half over as it did so.

The eagle could carry brant or ducks away bodily but when the booty was too large, the two birds went to the ground together, the eagle, in a sense, riding its victim.

The owner of the victor would then come and take up the prize, rehooding the captor until other game was sighted.

There are a few eagles in the United States being used as falcons today, and Broley often receives requests from lads or young men to help them obtain a young eagle to train. He refuses, of course. The training is a long, arduous one and only to be undertaken by men who know it fully. Charlie hates to see these fine birds in captivity. They will make gentle and devoted pets but require a great deal of food. Then, too, as they will fly to strangers for food, they are apt to hurt a person who does not understand what they are after, and then the bird may be hurt or even destroyed.

The northern bald eagle, *Haliaeetus Leucocephalus Alascanus*, while somewhat larger, is in temperament and habit much like this near relation, our southern bald eagle. Of male eagles measured in Alaska the average length of the wing was 24.07 inches, while the females averaged 25.54.

Males measured in New England and New York were 23.33, while females were 25.40. The males in Florida averaged about 20.83 and the females, 22.65.

Now and then an exceedingly large female will be found breeding in Florida, and Broley is of the opinion that she is a northern bird. He has one such female which nests not far from the city of Tampa. The offspring, usually two, are very much larger than other eaglets around there and, also, they are much more easily handled for they do not fight as the others do at the same age.

He was told that a man who formerly lived in Alaska had brought a large bald eagle back with him to this vicinity and that it had escaped. Possibly this is that bird.

In Ontario the nests are constructed much as they are in the south but are generally in well branched, tall elms. They do not contain anything like the same amount of lining nor do the male birds carry up the queer odds and ends that the southern species does.

While nests in Florida frequently contain a quantity of fish, often quite fresh, there is seldom anything except bones and other remains in Ontario nests.

In British Columbia and the south side of the Alaska Peninsula, the eagle nests in large trees, usually live spruce or hemlock. In the Aleutian Islands, they build their eyries on rocky cliffs or in pinnacles of rock. Sometimes these nests are quite easily reached, and Broley has had some pictures sent to him showing eggs and eaglets.

CHAPTER TWELVE

Eagles and Their Neighbors

MOST PEOPLE lucky enough to have an eagle's nest near them take a proud interest in it. With the boom in building in Florida in recent years, Broley found a number of houses built, or going up, near nests. The unusual activity drove the birds away in a few cases but some owners were able to keep them.

Eagles show a very strong attachment to a chosen territory. When a pair lose their nest or desert it after a disaster such as the young being killed or the nest robbed, they nearly always choose a tree near by for the new home. Sometimes, rather than leave the vicinity, they build in a tree unsuitable for the purpose, a weak tree or one with a very poor crotch. In the latter case they will occasionally put it up right on top of the tree. Some have been on branches not strong enough to support the heavy weight. Such nests seldom last more than a year; the first heavy wind takes them down.

A pair of eagles will often forego nesting rather than leave a district when their nest has been destroyed and no suitable place can be found for a new site.

Because of this attachment, a great deal of disturbance

may occur around a nest without causing the eagles to
leave. When Gadsden's Point near Tampa was taken over
by the Army Air Forces in 1941, there was an eagle's nest
on it. In 1942, a bombing target was located close to this
tree and planes zoomed in from all sides to drop "bombs"
but did not scare the eagles away. Of course these were
sacks of flour or non-explosives but the noise must have
been frightening.

I might add that the bander that year was almost struck
by such a bomb. He had permission to go onto the field
and, driving over near the nest, parked his car and walked
over to it. He had hardly gotten up into the tree before
jeeps and motor cycles roared up to the spot and angry
voices called out to know what he thought he was doing.

From his vantage point up in the nest he explained.
When they understood what it was all about permission
was soon given to continue. "But," he was cautioned, "next
time you come in here let us know. Why you might have
been killed. This is a bombing area and if one of these
things dropped from a plane hit you—"

In 1944, all the trees around the one containing the nest
were cut. Bulldozers and tractors created a constant disturbance near by and the daily target practice went on, but the
eagles stayed around though no eggs were laid.

A pair of eagles raised their young successfully year after
year in Sarasota right in the midst of a group of houses. The
ground dwellers were so proud of their neighbors above
that they at first refused permission to band the eaglets,
fearing this might cause the parents to abandon the site.
However, after they saw that broods were raised each

season in other nests where banding was done each January, they agreed to allow Broley to tag theirs also.

A new house going up beside a nesting spot had the permit right on the eagle's tree. The owner was worried lest the big birds might leave but Broley reassured him. There were young, about two weeks old, in the nest and he said, "The parents will have to feed the eaglets for nine weeks or so yet. They'll get used to you being around and, if they are not molested, will return next season."

Sure enough, the next year when he revisited that section, the owner met him jubilantly. "My eagles came back," he said, "they came on September tenth about seven in the evening. You know," he continued, "they were so glad to get back they kept us all awake—talked until three in the morning!"

A nest about five miles from St. Petersburg overlooked the Bay. A house was being built within one hundred and twenty feet of the nest tree in 1941, when the eagles returned to make ready for a new family. They would go to the nest every morning at dawn but left when the workmen arrived. Apparently it was all too much for them and the female did not lay that season. The owner, quite anxious for fear they would leave completely, asked Broley what he should do to coax them back. Broley suggested that work on the house be suspended during most of the next October. This was done and the eagles returned to their nest. For three seasons all went well; then a hurricane swept the eyrie from the tree and they did not rebuild there but chose a tree about half a mile away.

People who buy or lease property near a nest very soon

learn to watch the activities in and around it. They like to learn as much as possible about their non-paying tenants or neighbors. One of our friends who is lucky enough to be able to watch proceedings from her breakfast nook says she feels as if the babies belonged to her.

So much timber has been cut in Florida that good, substantial nesting trees are hard to find. One fine eyrie was in a big tree on a tract that was sold for lumber. The owner was very proud of this nest and stipulated that the tree in which it was located should not be felled when the tract was cut.

A week or so after felling had started he went out to see how things were going and was very angry when he discovered that in spite of his instructions the tree was down—of course the nest was not in use at that time.

"I'm terribly sorry," the lumberman assured him. "You just can't get these Negroes to do what they are told. Tell you what, though. You pick out a good tree, one that should suit the eagles and this time I'll make sure that it is left."

The owner of the tract picked out three trees and, to make sure that they were left, marked each with a tin sign which read "Reserved for eagles."

When, that fall, the birds returned, they saw the sign, accepted the reservation and built a fine new nest. Two grand eaglets were raised that year and the next.

Mr. Harry S. Slocum of St. Petersburg has a splendid eagle's nest near his home. He notes the arrival dates each fall and there is slight variation. In 1947 the pair returned on the fifteenth of August. In 1948 he did not see them until August 27th. In 1949 they were back on the twenty-fourth, but in 1950 they came quite early for he saw them on August 20th.

Mr. Slocum accompanied Charlie to a nest near the ferry at St. Petersburg on February 16th. Fire had swept through the area, burning the palmettos, and the tree containing the nest was burned almost three quarters of the way in.

While Charlie was taking his ladders out of the car, Mr. Slocum examined the tree. "Looks pretty hazardous," he said. "Do you think it is safe for you to go up?"

"Guess it's all right," Charlie said. "I'll chance it anyway."

He banded the young birds and came down safely. Later Mr. Slocum wrote him that the tree fell down on April 5th, and the two young were killed. Only about six inches of good wood was keeping the tree in place when Charlie climbed it.

Mr. and Mrs. E. B. Ball of Sarasota have a splendid big nest they can watch from their lawn or windows. Last fall the nest was still in good condition though the tree holding it was dead. The big birds decided to erect a new eyrie and chose a site in a live tree, only forty feet away—both trees are pines. The two eagles labored diligently, the male bringing in much material which the female placed in position. They even carried up masses of Spanish moss for the lining. Then, apparently, the female decided it was too much of an effort to move for she laid her eggs in the old nest after all. Charlie is hoping she will use the new nest this season; he could build a very handy blind on the top of the old one and get chances for exceptional pictures.

CHAPTER THIRTEEN

Migration and Returns

WHEN CHARLIE began his banding in January, 1939, few bald eagles had been banded in Florida. The southern subspecies was believed to be non-migratory. Of the forty-four eaglets he tagged that year, one was taken on May 8th, that same year, at Columbiaville, New York, more than eleven hundred miles from its nest. This was quite a surprise and might have been considered merely an exception but almost at once others were reported from the north, one getting up as far as King's County, Prince Edward Island, more than sixteen hundred miles from home.

It was decided to continue the banding to discover how far these birds traveled and, again, most of the returns were from the north. Some birds reach Canada within a few weeks of the time they first learn to fly.

With the exception of two recoveries made in Indiana and Illinois, those up to 1945 indicated a coastwise migration through Georgia, the Carolinas, and Virginia. In 1945, there were four inland recoveries, in Mississippi, Illinois, Michigan, and western New York. The explanation for these was a change that year in the prevailing winds, which, instead of moving up the Atlantic coast, blew across Florida towards the west and then north into the valley of the Mississippi. The young adventurers, taking advantage of these winds, went right along with them.

In 1947, the most astonishing recovery was that of a bird shot two hundred miles north of the city of Winnipeg, in Manitoba.

There were no recoveries north of Florida, of eagles banded there, in January, February, or March, and none in Florida between June and September in any year. This would go to show that at least the immature Florida bald eagle spends late summer and early fall in the north.

Broley has banded only one adult eagle and is not in Florida during the summer season, but a number of reliable observers have assured him that no eagles are to be seen there in July and very few during June or August. He believes that all the eagles leave the south during the warm months, returning with cooler weather. Also he believes that young birds may go right up to the Arctic in their wanderings.

Hawk Mountain near Kempton, Pennsylvania, has long been known to ornithologists as a wonderful ridge from which to observe migrating birds. Some twelve thousand hawks and two hundred or so eagles drift past during the fall migration there. Unfortunately, this spot was known to hunters also and every October several hundred ruthless gunners would take this opportunity of trying out their skill at these splendid targets.

To naturalists this senseless slaughter was a tragedy and thanks to the untiring efforts of Mrs. C. N. Edge of New

CLIMBING TO AN EAGLE'S NEST

U. S. Air Force Photo

EAGLETS FROM NEST AT U. S. ARMY AIR F

BROLEY AND TWO EAGL

Photo by Nelson Edwards

BROLEY AND 3-WEEK-OLD BALD EAGLE

ADULT BALD EAGLE IN FLORIDA

Photo by Nelson Edwards

BANDING YOUNG EA

MYRTLE J. BROLEY AND EAGLET

BROLEY UP AT NEST

ULT AND YOUNG EAGLES   ADULT EAGLES AT NEST

Photos by Dr. Charles Proctor

EAGLET: PHOTO-
GRAPHED FROM NEST
80 FEET UP

EAGLET: 12 WEEKS OLD

EAGLET: ON N

EAGLETS: 9 WEEKS OLD

HEAD OF EAGLET: II WEEKS OLD

ADULT BALD EAGLE

by Dr. Charles Proctor

BROLEY AND RICHARD H. PO

York City this area was finally declared a sanctuary. Now people from all over may go there to watch the aerial manoeuvres of these birds and rejoice that they are safe from shot and shell. A flight of from two to three thousand may be seen in a day, a wonderful picture as they pass below the watchers, drifting along on air currents with almost motionless wings.

The addition of a number of bald and golden eagles added interest to the spectacle, the bald, appearing first during the last week in August, with the largest numbers going over in September.

Now the bald eagle is a hardy bird and appears quite indifferent to temperatures well below zero. Many observers wondered why so many eagles were moving south so early. They never suspected that they were Florida birds hurrying back to claim their old nests after spending the hottest days in the north. Broley first discovered the northward summer movement by the bald eagle after his banded youngsters began turning up in New York, Maine, and Canada.

Now ornithologists feel sure that the bulk of the Hawk Mountain eagle flight comprises these southern birds.

Many of the adult northern bald eagles do not migrate south at all if the winter is mild. They may go for January and part of February when the season is exceedingly cold and food is scarce. The immature quite probably spend a longer period in the warmer regions.

The southern bald eagle is slightly smaller than the northern species. Prior to Broley's banding many museums in the north contained mounted eagles differing considerably in size. They were all listed as *Haliaeetus Alascanus* but the curators were puzzled by the variations in measurements. Some were so much smaller than others. Now they have relisted these small birds as *Haliaeetus Leucocephalus Leucocephalus*, the southern eagle.

It is an unfortunate thing that most of the recoveries are of birds that have been shot, caught in traps, or similar tragedies. It would be hard to devise a means of catching an adult eagle at the nest which would not result in damage to the bird, or to eggs, or young. Broley has come up onto a nest just as a parent returned from a hunting trip and, on one such occasion, was sure he could have caught the big creature by its talons but was afraid to try lest the small young be knocked off the nest or injured. That he might have been hurled from the nest himself did not seem to enter his thoughts.

Young eagles he has banded in Canada have been taken in a number of southern states during December, but he thinks that in mild winters adults do not leave the north at all or, if they do, go only a short distance. Trappers and lumbermen will tell him about seeing the grand big birds around almost all winter. They often use their nests as a feeding station or lookout perch.

An interesting sight in Florida is a group of young, dark, immature birds with possibly one or two white-headed ones all together in a large field near Largo.

Practically all Broley's recoveries have been of birds banded that year. He has several theories for this. He thinks that hunters may possibly mistake the young bird, which is all dark, for a large hawk. This is no excuse, of course, for many of our largest hawks are the most beneficial.

He would like to believe that no one would willingly shoot a bald eagle. Then, too, he wonders if the eaglet becomes warier with age, learning to keep away from predatory men. He wonders also whether they could get the firm, strong bands off, as some people have suggested. He plans to bracelet his young eagles with a new locking band which would certainly stay for life. Eagles might pick at the band when it was first put on but it would soon become a commonplace to them, making no difference to the talon.

Eagles are often caught in muskrat or fox traps, either attracted by the bait or the captured animal. When the talon has been injured by one of these wretched things it may never regain its strength.

Raymond Conway, of Placida, who patrolled a 28,000-acre tract twice a week, kept a record for Broley of adult eagles seen during July and August between 1941 and 1945. In 1941 he did not see any, nor in 1944 or 1945. In 1942, he saw two fine birds during this time and in 1943, he saw one. Early on the morning of September 7th, 1944, he saw twenty-seven adult eagles sitting about in dead trees on an island not far from his house, the first eagles he had seen that year since the month of June.

Mrs. Kathryn Reagle, who has an eyrie on her property a mile south of Sarasota, reported that her birds, absent during late summer, returned on September twelfth in 1942, September fifteenth in 1943 and September third in 1945. In 1944 they were very late returning, no sign of them at all until October first.

Mr. and Mrs. G. W. Marett of Sarasota live four hundred feet from an eagle's nest. They report that on May 14th, 1944, about forty-five or fifty eagles soared over their house and took their eaglets away with them, going off in a northerly direction. They did not see them again until September 18th.

On August 1st, 1945, Roger Tory Peterson and Captain Frank McCamey visited Merritt Island, a haunt of the bald eagle on the east coast, and were unable to find a single eagle in a whole day's search.

Reports from others clearly indicate an absence of eagles during July and August, with September as the average date of return. Concentrations of birds, presumably migrants, have been reported during September.

Migrating southward with the bald eagles each fall over Hawk Mountain some sixty or seventy golden eagles add interest and a new mystery for the watchers. Where do they come from? Where are they going?

There is no known concentration of nesting golden eagles in North America, apart from those in the Rockies. A few used to build their eyries in the Smokies but Doctor Walter R. Spofford, who has made a study of this bird, says he has not seen any of their nests in recent years.

The birds that wing past Hawk Mountain surely cannot be from the Rockies, but where have they reared their young? Labrador, northern Quebec, or Ontario might be possibilities but we do not know. Where do they spend the winters?—they are not heard of again after they migrate over Pennsylvania.

Here is a project for some young ornithologist to work on. Young, because it may take several years, and Broley at seventy-one does not feel able to undertake it. His work with the bald eagle will keep him busy for a few years yet.

CHAPTER FOURTEEN

Hurricanes

As so many of the eyries are near the water, the storms of early autumn cause considerable havoc; nests are blown out of trees, and in some cases the trees are uprooted. When the storm has been severe, the eagles will be so disturbed that no eggs are laid or, if they are, they will not be fertile.

The hurricane of October 17th-18th, in 1944, was quite upsetting to the big birds. The first survey of the nests was made by Broley about the end of November. Almost all had been damaged, some much more than others. Eighteen of the nesting trees under observation had been torn up by the roots and about half of the other nests had been blown out of the trees.

With but one exception all these nests were rebuilt, most of them with sticks that had been in the original structure; about the only time an eagle takes branches from the ground is in a case like this. There was still plenty of time for normal nesting and Broley thought everything would be all right. But that was not the case.

In twenty-four of the rebuilt nests no eggs were laid, although the mated pair were seen almost daily at the eyrie or in the vicinity.

In twenty-one nests the eggs did not hatch, although the birds incubated for two months. It was interesting to watch the birds towards the end of this sixty-day period. One would go to the nest, settle carefully on the eggs and incubate for about fifteen minutes or so, then fly off. The mate would then fly over, settle down on the eggs, often turning them over first, and spend ten or twelve minutes warming them up, then go off and join the other eagle on a near-by tree. They would remain perched there for half an hour or so before resuming these sporadic sessions.

Under normal conditions fifty-four young birds would have been produced from these forty-five nests, so this one hurricane caused a greater loss through non-production than the mortality caused by man in six years.

It was interesting to learn from poultry raisers in the district that hens did not lay for three weeks after the hurricane and that they seemed to have lost their desire to incubate. Great horned owls also seemed upset in their schedules.

Professor F. B. Hutt of Cornell University suggested that disturbances will cause a drop in egg production. Often unfavorable changes in the environment will cause the large ova, still attached to the ovary, to degenerate and then be resorbed. He believes that if, at the time of the storm, eagles had ova well advanced, there might have been resorption and the development of new ova might have upset the normal reproductive cycle.

He went on to say that laying a daily egg is little in the life of a good domestic fowl, but for the eagle, which lays two only in the year, the chain of physiological processes leading up to it might be a long one.

If gales blow during the season when eaglets are in the nest, Broley worries away for fear some of them will be blown out. He had one nest that was rather exposed, and one Tuesday evening he wakened during such a storm and said, "I'm afraid the bird in the nest on Manatee in Bradenton will be blown out tonight."

Not until Friday was he able to get down to that tree and, sure enough, there was the young eaglet on the ground. It had little fight left and seemed very thin. He climbed up to the nest with it and as soon as he placed it on top of the big mound it scuttled over to a fine big fish lying there and began to eat, paying no attention to the rescuer at all.

Eagles will bring food to the eyrie even after the young are able to fly about, but they will not feed them on the ground.

There have been lesser hurricanes since the one of 1944 but they have done little damage to nests or trees in the area where Broley bands. They might, however, have been a factor in the non-production of eggs in certain nests.

Charlie discovered an interesting nest in February, 1945. This was in the district where the 1944 hurricane had blown so many nests out of their trees. A pair of birds evidently decided to guard against the disaster. They found a tree which had branches reaching out from all around the trunk at one level, forty-two feet up, like the spokes in a large wagon wheel.

The birds built their nest completely about the trunk,

giving it three or four feet of space all around. The eggs could have been incubated on any side of it.

This feature was a very happy one for the young before they were fully covered with the second type of down. The tiny fellows must have shade or the intense heat of the sun in Florida will kill them. In this nest, as the sun moved around the tree, the young could advance into the shade and so have continual protection throughout the day, and the parents did not have to stand over them in the hottest periods. That the sun is indeed scorching there is borne out by the proven fact that a rattlesnake, left unshaded in it during July, will die in thirty minutes.

CHAPTER FIFTEEN

Observation of Young Eagles
from the Blind

To WATCH the parents from the ground was all right, but when Charlie decided to study and photograph the young birds he realized that he would need to be up on a level with them, or even slightly higher than they were. He planned to build several blinds up in trees which were near nests and so get the young ones at different stages. He was particularly anxious to obtain pictures of the parents feeding the young eaglets.

It was no easy task to carry material up into trees and then build while hanging on, some seventy feet off the ground. His first such "study" was over near Clearwater and he soon discovered that getting into a hide on the ground without the adults seeing him was a simple matter compared with trying to do the same thing up in a tree. He went in several mornings before daybreak, but the birds saw him even so and, although he stayed there for the rest of the day, the old pair did not come near the eyrie. He had a splendid chance to watch the young ones, but of course would not be able to stay very long while they were still small, lest they become chilled in cold weather or sunburned when it was too hot.

It is nice to watch the parents cuddle the little ones during a chilly spell or when it rains. At a time like that one realizes what a devoted parent the eagle is. The babies need to be fed often, like other small creatures but the older eaglets can go for lengthy periods without food and show no noticeable distress.

Almost all birds and animals are nervous when fire breaks out near them. On one occasion when a fire roared through the palmettos past an eyrie, Charlie noticed that the mother eagle murmured soothingly to the young bird all the time, just as a parent would try to reassure a child. He found it most touching.

Eaglets do not play about in the nest as much as some of the larger birds do, although it is the opinion of some naturalists that the queer objects found in eagle nests may have been brought there as playthings for the young. They do pull at sticks or move them about in the nest, even picking up things and tossing them in the air. When they are about seven weeks old they begin learning to fly or, at least, begin to strengthen their wing muscles by exercising them. As they grow older they spend more and more time at this. On a breezy day they may be seen moving their black wings up and down, even jumping up and down a little as if testing them out. Once in awhile an eaglet will jump right over its nest mate.

This jumping looks most amusing; the long feathers give the bird the appearance of wearing "droopy pants" as it leaps up and down.

They hear the parent coming in with food long before the watcher in the blind sees or hears. An alert expression, the tilt of the young bird's head, gives the first signal. This proved a great help in photography for Charlie could get his camera ready and be able to catch the mother as she came in with food.

As she came nearer, the young birds jumped up and down, squealed and pushed each other as if to say "I want this. It's my turn." One bigger eaglet pushed her little brother so hard at a time like this that he went right over on his back and did not seem to recover from the blow for some little time after that. She was successful in getting all the food the parent brought in and the poor, small eagle did not get even a taste. Sometimes the eaglets run to the edge of the nest and peer over like eager children.

The sound of the camera often bothers the adults, especially the male, and the food is dropped whole. If not alarmed, however, the parent will stay an hour or more, watching them feed, helping tear up the fish or animal brought in.

Sometimes a young eaglet decides to fix up the home a bit. There was a stub sticking out from the centre of a nest and a little fellow worked away trying to pull it out. Quite often he would tug so hard that he'd lose his balance and turn a somersault, landing on his back.

Charlie had sat for two days in one blind with no luck in photographing the parents at all. They just did not come near the nest. He wasn't just satisfied with his quarters so he thought he would fix them up a little. The third day then, knowing that he would be making a lot of noise with the lumber and saw he took in, he did not bother taking along his camera.

He worked away zealously and made his repairs. Just as he finished, the mother eagle came into the nest with a merganser, a fish-eating duck which sportsmen scorn. She sat at the edge of the nest and plucked it, and the feathers went off in a stream. He said he had never seen one plucked so fast. Then she tore the duck up and fed the children and all the time he sat there, facing her, without a camera! He regretted most of all the picture he would have gotten when the young birds, grabbing it, tried to swallow it. It could not get the webbed foot down, however, and this was waggled back and forth in a most ludicrous manner as the young chap gulped and swallowed.

Down near Englewood Charlie found a nest and a tree about forty feet away from which he could photograph. Unfortunately, although he was able to rig up the blind, there was no way of making a floor for it, nor was there anything on which he could sit. He thought a sort of swing made by fastening up some wire would be enough—he does not mind discomfort—so he purchased some wire which the salesman told him was good and strong.

After getting the blind ready, Charlie left it for three weeks so that the adults would be accustomed to it and he could get pictures of them feeding the young.

He drove the eighty miles down to it the night before, so that he could get in very early in the morning, and slept in his car. When he walked in, very early the next morning, he found that a windstorm the day before had blown the baby out of the nest. He had to put up his ladders and take this eaglet back to its home, then get them down and put them up to his own shelter. By this time, of course, the parent eagles were thoroughly disturbed and he knew it would be some time before either one came in with food.

About four o'clock in the afternoon, when he had been waiting for about eight hours, he saw the young one begin to act as if the parent were coming. He leaned forward to see and just at that moment the "strong" wire broke and he went backwards out of the blind. Fortunately he managed to swing himself in towards the tree trunk, grasping the stub of a branch about six feet below his blind, and pulled himself into the tree. As he says, he "certainly scared the wits out of the eagle."

His camera had been wired up to the tree so he hadn't had the worry of that. Knowing there would be no further chance of a picture that day, he repaired his swing and then went to band a nest a little further south.

The next day he broke a rear axle in heavy sand. That week end a lady called him on the telephone and said, "I hear you've been having bad luck. Is it true that you fell out of a tree and broke your rear axle?"

CHAPTER SIXTEEN

Excitement in Banding

ONE OF the questions most frequently asked Charlie is: "Don't the adult eagles attack you? Aren't they very vicious?"

To date they have not attacked him, although several times they have come very close to it. The first time he bands young in a nest he is very careful; it is then that the parents swoop the lowest and scream most defiantly. He believes they know him after that and realize that he will not harm the young. Still, they do stoop at him and the swish of their great wings is very loud.

Young birds often attack him ferociously while he is putting on the band. They use their talons mostly, although the beak is employed at times also. He likes to bracelet them when they are between three and five weeks old. Then the band is not proportionately so large that it could fall off over the toes which develop very quickly on the eaglet; and also, they aren't able to tear Charlie up so much. However, if he finds a new nest in which there are large, dark young, he will attempt to band them as long as they are not able to fly completely out of sight.

Often a bird of nine or ten weeks of age will plane off

and down from its nest, to land quite a distance away. He marks the spot as well as he can, descends, and hunts it up again, for he knows it will not be able to take off from the ground and would starve if left there. The parents will continue to bring food to the nest long after the young birds are flying about, and they will return to the eyrie to get it. But birds do not seem to realize that young that tumble from the nest need to be fed.

Charlie has to go up and down his trees quite often sometimes. At first, he used to tie the eagle up in a sack to take it back when it tumbled or planed out. Now he fastens the talons together, attaches a long rope to this fastener, and climbs to the nest. Once there, he hauls the bird up. Since it is more or less on its back, it doesn't struggle and there is no danger of its getting hurt. Even alone at a nest, he can get the eaglet up safely this way.

Going in to the nests, he has to watch for rattlers and they may even be near the tree. When he used to spread his nylon cord out so that it would run freely as he tossed the weight, he had at least one narrow escape.

On this occasion, there were a couple of men with him and they sat down near by while he got things ready. He spread the canvas out, noticing as he did so a near-by palmetto. Then he moved his hands back and forth, placing the cord. When all was in readiness, he stepped back to get a better view of the crotch through which he planned to toss the weight. He felt his foot go on something soft and jumped a couple of feet in the air. He had been standing on a rattler concealed under a frond of the palmetto!

Fortunately, he must have been right on its neck. When

he yelled, the men with him could not at first make out the snake, so cleverly was it concealed and camouflaged. They made short work of killing it, though, and agreed that it must have been well fed, and therefore, sluggish. Charlie's hand, spreading the line, had been only inches from it several times.

The rattlesnake as a rule will not attack unless alarmed. A grove owner told me that, one day, as he was walking through his trees, he was watching a bird up in the grape fruit branches. As it flew from place to place, he moved back and forth to see it better. He had walked back and forth along a stretch three times and was just starting back again when he glanced down and saw a large rattler stretched out midway. The snake knew as soon as he had seen it for it coiled at once and began to rattle warningly. Yet he had passed very close to it on the other trips.

Near another of his nests the owner of the land over which Charlie had to tramp in warned him to be on the watch for snakes. "I killed eighty-three rattlers around this grove the first fifteen months I was here," he said.

As Charlie's path led in through thick scrub he knew there were very likely many more lurking about. He prefers to wear tennis shoes with rubber soles for climbing and had been walking in to the trees and back with these on. Now he uses high boots for the worst spots, changing to the others before he starts up the tree.

Moccasins or cottonmouths are encountered near or in water. Now that so many of the pines have been cut, eagles are building back in the cypress trees. This makes it a little harder for Charlie since many of these trees are much higher than the pines and moreover the ground around them is very often swampy, if not actually covered with water.

He was going over to one of these cypress-tree nests and had crossed part of the water. Noticing a log just ahead, he decided to walk on it to get over a deeper place. Just as he went to put his foot on it, he glimpsed a bit of white through the murky water just below. Looking more closely, he was able to make out the open, light-colored mouth from which this reptile gets its name. One more step and the poisonous thing would have had him.

In Florida they cross Brahma cattle from India with other breeds. The Brahmas, being heat and tick resistant, do better in this climate and the cross makes a better beef animal. Bulls of this hybrid breed are often very fierce, and on one occasion Broley had to climb a tree in a hurry to get away from one. The cows with calves are a menace also and chase anyone coming around.

Catclaw vines tear him up when he has to push his way in through their tangles, and he gets covered with ticks, burrs, and so forth.

When he began this work he was, at times, taken for a "Revenue Man" and grass fires were set which almost burned his car, twice. Now he tries to let everyone in the neighborhood know what he is doing and if at all possible, even though it may necessitate a long walk carrying all his gear, he leaves his car in someone's yard so that it won't be in this danger. Grass and palmetto fires do a lot of damage during very dry seasons and many of the trees containing nests have been partially burned.

Excitement in Banding

Mr. Mack Doss, a rancher down below Sarasota, was very proud of an eagle's nest on his property. He was always warning people to keep away from it and made sure no one got close enough to injure the birds.

In July one year, after the eagles had left for the north, Mr. Doss was burning off some scrub not far from this tree. He had just turned to start for home when he heard a crackling. Looking back he discovered that the fire had run along through dried grass, gone up the tree trunk, and set the big nest with its dry sticks and roots ablaze. He told us it really was a spectacular sight, this bonfire in the sky, but he felt very badly to think he had caused this and was afraid the eagles would not come back around there. However, the pair returned in late August, built a new nest, and raised a pair of eaglets.

One of Charlie's nests which contained two young eagles was in a tree up which fire had run almost to the nest. They left the nest safely and the pair moved to a new site the next fall.

At the close of one banding season, Charlie had his worst fall; he had decided to put his remaining bands away in an upper cupboard and did what he has so often warned me against doing; he got up on a chair instead of taking time to get the stepladder. As he stretched up, the chair overturned and he went to the floor with a thud, striking his chin on the end of the bed as he did so, and knocking himself out completely.

When people shudder as he swings from limb to limb in tall trees, I often tell them that he says he is safer there than on the ground.

A very good friend of his, Mr. R. C. Laidlaw, had a venom laboratory near Ruskin. He could handle the big rattlers with little concern, apparently, as he held them over a glass to catch the deadly poison they ejected, poison which can be used to alleviate fevers, to make serums, and so forth.

Mr. Laidlaw asked Charlie one day when he stopped in if he was on the way to band the eaglets in a near-by nest.

"Yes," Charlie said. "Do you want to come along?"

"If you'll wait until I milk these two snakes I will," Laidlaw said. "Thought I might climb up and take a look at the nest if it's all right with you."

"Fine," Charlie answered and watched with interest as the milking continued.

"Like to try doing it?" Mr. Laidlaw asked. "You put your fingers right at the back of the head like this but keep them very firm. You know a snake can turn its head inside the skin so you have to be careful." He moved off a little so that Charlie could get in closer to the reptile.

"No thank you!" Charlie said, backing away. "That's something I don't want to learn about."

Soon after that they went over to the tree. Charlie got the ladders up and said: "Would you like to go up first?" Mr. Laidlaw started up the ladder, got about eighteen feet, and then came back down.

"You can have your tree climbing," he said when he reached the earth again, "I'll stick to the rattlers and deep-sea diving."

Broley is frequently asked if he has ever fallen out of a

tree. Here in his own words is the story of an experience that almost ended fatally.

"We were looking for a nest on Devil Lake in Frontenac County in Ontario and were traveling up along the west shore with the motor on the boat running slowly. The shoreline ran up very abruptly to a height of eighty feet and soon I noticed a nest in the top of a tree that stood out well above all the other timber.

"That tree must be growing right on top of the ridge, I thought, until I came closer and saw that it was a soft elm or swamp elm, a species which never grows on rocky ridges but has its roots in low places, usually close to, or right in, the swamps. I immediately realized it must be a very high tree to reach from water level well over the top of the eighty-foot ridge.

"Landing our boat we climbed the ridge and then dropped down into the low land where we came to the foot of the tree holding the nest. It was indeed a splendid tree and the nest, under actual measurement, was ninety-five feet from the ground. This meant a stiff climb, which made it all the more interesting for there is no thrill or excitement in mounting an easy tree.

"Reaching the nest, I foolishly got up on it without examining the underpinning. In this case three quarters of the big structure was supported by a dead limb, which broke off as soon as my weight was added to the nest, allowing it to tip down at an angle of about forty-five degrees. The young eagle was obliged to dig in its talons to keep from sliding off and I would certainly have gone if I had not had a good grip on a strong branch behind me.

"I thought, 'This will never do, to break down the only nest on Devil Lake.' I usually take a strong, heavy cord up with me to every nest. I doubled this and got it under the eyrie, hoping that it would be sufficient support until the next day when I intended to come back and prop the nest up again.

"Fortunately there was no wind during the night to wholly displace the structure and it was still there when we arrived with repairs the next morning.

"I brought several two-by-fours, eight feet long, with me as well as some ten-inch spikes. I wired a pulley up behind the nest to the limb that had saved me the previous day, got a big rope around and under the nest, ran it through the pulley and dropped it to the ground where the two strong chaps I had brought with me pulled on it and slowly raised the nest up to its original position.

"I then spiked my two-by-fours under the nest in such a way as to give it good support again. Now it is good for another twenty-five years.

"However, it occurred to me that, when the leaves fell off in the autumn and the duck hunters went out on the lake and saw those big timbers under the nest, there would be some tall stories going around as to the ability of eagles to carry up heavy nesting material."

CHAPTER SEVENTEEN

Nests, Courtship, and Eggs

WHEN EAGLES return to their nesting tree the last week of September or early in October, they immediately begin repair work. Some years they add as much as two feet of new material.

The nests of these Florida eagles are, in general, much higher from top to bottom than those of northern birds. The largest Ontario nest that Charlie has under observation is eight feet wide and eight feet high. His largest Florida nest, one near St. Petersburg, is twenty feet deep and nine and a half feet wide.

Size and shape depend on the kind of tree in which the eyrie rests. In many Florida pines the crotches are very deep, giving plenty of support so the nest can be built higher each year. Most of the Ontario nests are in elms which have outspreading crotches so they tend to be wide, rather than deep. Now that so many pines have been cut, more eagles will have to go to the cypress swamps in Florida to nest and, as they have wide-spreading crotches, new nests will be wider.

The widest nest Broley has under observation in Florida is in a cypress which has a girth of twenty-two feet. The eyrie, about one hundred and fifteen feet from the ground, is almost ten feet across and five feet deep.

When a nest is wide, like this, it is hard to tell from the ground just what is in it. From most nests, the white head of an incubating eagle can be seen over the top of the structure, and when she is brooding small chicks, the raised wings are visible, but if she is in the very centre of an extremely wide nest, nothing at all can be seen.

So many trees have been cut in the Boca Grande district that Broley has found three nests built in mangroves, only about twelve feet from the ground. Quite a comedown, this, from the lordly heights to which they are accustomed.

In Ontario, the eagles usually choose tall elms in which to build. Here again nests are found, as a rule, near lakes or streams.

The eagle does not pick up fallen branches for nesting material but gets the bough right off the tree. Charlie has seen them fly at a chosen limb with great speed and break it right off. Again, they will sometimes fold their wings and drop onto the branch from a height, cracking it cleanly. Of course these are dead branches but they are still strong.

When winds or hurricanes blow the nest out of the tree or blow part of it off, then the eagle retrieves his first construction pieces from the ground when he starts the new nest.

An eagle was observed, one day, flying in to an island with a good-sized branch of a tree. The nearest land with trees was five miles distant; she had really worked for her lumber that day.

Many nests are known to have been in use for decades

but neither of the original pair may survive. The eagle, unlike geese, swans, and some other large birds, will take a new mate very soon after the old one is killed, although they do mate for life. The survivor then brings this new companion to the old nest and they continue to use it. Ownership is passed along in this way.

Near Sarasota there was a tall pine in which eagles had nested for many years. One by one houses were built near this spot and the owners were justly proud of their avian neighbors.

When Charlie found this nest for the first time there were only three houses near by. One of these belonged to Judge Chapman, a real nature lover who was afraid the banding of the young might disturb the adults or injure the eaglets. He objected to Charlie climbing up and as he could see that the judge was very interested he did not try, although he was quite sure he could have insisted on his right to do so.

The next spring, when he visited the nest again to see if he could band the young, Judge Chapman was still pretty irascible on the subject.

"You will have to obtain permission from the Chief of Police of Sarasota before you climb that tree," he declared.

"I have it," Charlie replied. "I telephoned from the home of the gentleman who lives in that house. Judge," Charlie went on, "the rougher you get with me the better I like it and the more I think of you. You are the kind of a conservationist I like to find living near an eagle's nest. It is safe under your protection." He was turning, ready to go away, when the Judge said, "Oh well! Guess you know what you're doing. Might as well climb up. I'd like to know if anything happens to those two eagles, though I certainly hope nothing does."

Lightning struck this tree in November, 1940, killing the incubating eagle. The male mated again and they continued to use the nest. In the spring of 1944 there were two fine young birds in the nest but one got only as far north as Ringtown, Pennsylvania, being picked up dead on the third of June.

During July, 1946, a houseowner near by was burning trash near the tree when the fire got away and ran right up the tree. The big nest was burned up. When the mated pair returned that fall they began building operations in a tree about two hundred feet away, and this fine eyrie is still in use.

This is the nest to which Charlie took Doctor Arthur A. Allen a number of years ago when he wanted to take some pictures of adult eagles. A fairly tame bird was necessary and this female could hardly be driven away. To get his pictures, taken from the ground with a telephoto lens, Dr. Allen did not need any blind. In fact he would call to Charlie, "Hit the tree with a stick again, will you, and drive her off. I want to get another flight shot."

Mrs. Allen and I had gone along with the men and had watched for awhile as they photographed. When she saw that her husband was getting splendid chances for poses, Elsa Allen suggested that I go with her to see a friend in Sarasota.

We were away quite awhile and returned to find the men almost as busy as when we left. "Oh Arthur," Mrs.

Allen said, "I thought you'd be all finished. Did you get what you wanted?"

"I got quite a few pictures but not the one I hoped for," Dr. Allen replied, "the eagle just wouldn't coöperate."

I guess I looked quite surprised; certainly Charlie did, for this was one of his best trees at which to get pictures and he had thought the eagle had been most obliging.

"What picture did you want?" I asked.

"I wanted a picture of the eagle coming in," there was a twinkle in the doctor's eye, "with the flag of the United States in one talon and a bunch of arrows in the other, and," he shook his head mournfully, "she wouldn't coöperate. Otherwise," he grinned at our joyous shouts, "I got everything I could ask for."

Roger Tory Peterson, who paints such beautiful bird pictures, spent ten days with us in Florida. He was to do an article about Charlie for *Life* and was getting the pictures.

Charlie had written him sometime before to suggest that he practice raising himself off the ground, holding on to a bar, to strengthen his wrists. Charlie himself practices this "chinning the bar" from time to time so that he is sure he is in good condition for climbing. He says he knows that when he can go up sixteen times consecutively he is ready to tackle a tree.

For Mr. Peterson Charlie had chosen a nest near Englewood as being the best for the pictures he required. They both got up into the tree and Charlie tied Mr. Peterson to a strong branch where he could lean back and get some support. He told Peterson he did so in order to free his hands for photography but I know he was afraid that Tory, who becomes so enthusiastic, might forget, when he wanted to get a shot at a certain angle, that he was up in a tree.

Every bird lover who goes to Florida tries to take one of the Audubon tours from Lake Okeechobee. We were no exceptions and made the journey down in March of 1947.

It was a splendid trip; we saw a great many birds; sand-hill cranes were numerous, of course, as well as most of the herons, many rails, and clouds of ibises.

Dick Pough was leading tours that year as well as Alexander Sprunt. Our finest sight, of course, was seeing thousands of glossy ibis flying in to their roosting trees for the night. As they came in long lines, their dark bodies etched against the glow of the sunset sky, I was sure I had never seen anything lovelier. We were out on the lake where we had a splendid view and Mr. and Mrs. Edwin Way Teale and Dick were with us. We had gone out earlier than necessary so that I could see, and hear, a limpkin, that bird like an overgrown rail which many of the natives of Florida call the "crying bird" because of its peculiar, mournful cry.

Mr. Teale who, with his wife, had been taking pictures of birds around Okeechobee said he would like very much to see Charlie go up a tree to band an eaglet. There was a fine nest in the vicinity so it was arranged that we would all go over to it early the next morning.

When we started off we were chased by a herd of Brahmas which added to the fun. In the nest Charlie found one of the most aggressive young eleven-week-old birds he has had to handle. It was so difficult to band that it provided considerable entertainment for the spectators.

Contrary to what many people believe, the young do not come back to the old nest after maturity. They may hang around for awhile with the parents after their return from the north but are chased away when the eggs are laid for the season, if not before. We do, often, see them fly over a nest when we are at it and wonder if they are looking over their new brother or sister to see how they compare with the previous year's crop.

Like so many of our larger birds, swan, geese, cranes and so forth, the paired eagles remain together and only death breaks the bond. Once the mate has gone, however, the survivor soon chooses a new companion and the courtship, though brief, is ardent. Rapid chasing flights may often be seen in late September and through October. Evolutions high in the air are often seen.

Charlie had gone to one of his nests in late December to see what the birds were doing and, as he neared the tree, two white-headed birds flew up and away. He thought that nest could be written off for, had they been using it, they would have stayed to scold him and flown about. Walking over to the tree, he found a mature eagle lying dead at its foot.

Now, in the warm climate of Florida, decay sets in very promptly and this bird was still quite fresh so he was sure that it had not been dead for more than two or three days. It had been shot.

Just then he heard an eagle scream and, looking up, saw one of the two he had observed before chasing the other.

Suddenly they came together, locking talons and executed four complete cartwheels, tumbling down several hundred feet before breaking apart.

He was sure that one of the pair was the erstwhile mate of the dead eagle and that it had already chosen its new spouse. He has been lucky enough to see this courtship manoeuvre three times. Doctor Arthur Allen of Cornell has seen it once, and a number of other naturalists have told us about seeing it.

Broley says he has only once seen an immature eagle, that is, one that had not quite attained the full adult plumage, mated with a white-headed, white-tailed bird. He has never seen two immature birds mated nor has he heard of such an instance.

There was a nest near Gibsonton in which, although each year the female laid two eggs and incubated them for about two months, there were never young: the eggs were infertile.

One January when Charlie approached the place he was surprised to see two black heads in the nest, young birds of about four weeks.

He stopped to speak to the people residing near by and said, "Well, I see you have young birds this year all right."

"Yes," the man replied, "and we want to ask you a question about that. One day when the tide was out we heard screams from the eagles and saw them having a terrific fight in the air. Then they dropped to the ground over there and after awhile one got up and flew away. When the tide was in again we got the boat out and rowed over. There we found the other eagle, dead.

"Soon after that we saw two eagles repairing that nest and, as you see, they have young for the first time." He looked at Charlie intently, then continued, "What we'd like to know is, did that one eagle get fed up with the other and kill it off so she could take a new mate and produce young? We were sure the one that flew off was the larger and you told us that was the female."

Broley says he would like to know the answer also. All that he knows about it is that there are young in that nest each season now.

There may be quite a delay after the first egg is laid before the female deposits the second one in the nest, so sometimes one young bird is noticeably larger than the other. The eggs are small for the size of the bird, being only about twice the size of a hen's egg. They are chalky white and more oval than an owl's. Once in awhile an egg will be found with a few traces of pale brown or buff markings. These are not nest stains, which of course are common, but genuine coloring.

Incubation takes thirty-five days and the newly hatched young are helpless, fluffy, little greyish-white creatures. This light down grows out and soon the little fellow is covered with an almost fur-like covering of darkish grey woolly down.

The talons are large and at three weeks are almost full size. These are used by the young bird in fighting, rather than the beak.

One day when Charlie was trying to hold a nervous eaglet, bent on leaving the nest, and band the more aggressive female, she got her talons deeply into his hand. He had a hook around the other bird and was able to kneel on the end of this while he tried to pull the claw out, even using the pliers with which he tightens the bands, all to no avail.

In his efforts he got his head down too low and she managed to get her other talon into his face and head. He says his skull was too thick and, although she did gash him deeply, he managed to get it out. Blood was streaming down his face from the cuts beside his eyes and he doesn't know just how he got the other claw loosened. However, he did, and got her banded. He makes sure now to keep his face out of the way. We measured the marks of the talons on his face and found that the spread was seven and a half inches.

In the nests of bald eagles of the north, it is not unusual to find three eggs. In only two of his one hundred and twenty-five nests under observation in Florida would he hope to find three eggs or birds. One of these is the very big nest over near St. Petersburg and the other is a nest about a mile south of Ruskin. Usually nests contain two eggs; often only one.

He groups the users of his Florida nests under two headings, "early nesters" and "late nesters." The first begin laying early in November, the others in mid-December or even later. He finds that individuals are pretty consistent about laying time. Certain nests he must visit early in January or the young will be too large to handle easily. Others he does not check on till late February because the eaglets are never large enough to band before that time. He has one nest at Myaaka where the female is very late in laying her set, and these are so late in hatching that even when he leaves in April the young are too small to tag.

He has discovered that the early nesting birds produce two young much more frequently than the late nesters do. Whether this is because the latter lay only one egg or that only one egg is fertile, he is not sure.

Heat may be a factor in this; he finds that when the winter season is unusually warm, there are fewer young eagles. Of course very cold spells take their toll, also, especially if the sitting female is disturbed or kept off the eggs too long.

He went to a nest near St. Petersburg in cool weather and found that a troop of Scouts had built a camp right under the nest tree. It had turned very cold the day before and he was afraid the parent eagles, who were flying around scolding, had been kept off the eggs.

He told the boys they would have to move their camp at once. They were quite upset because they had spent a lot of time and effort fixing it up. He decided that he would climb up and look the situation over first.

There in the nest were two little dead eaglets, not yet fully out of the shells. The boys had evidently arrived just as the young chipped the shell and the parents had gone off. The cold had been too much for the little mites.

Breaking up camp would have been useless then, so Broley told them they could remain. However, they assured him they would be very careful in the future and not do anything like that again.

The eyes of young eagles are dark and we have been asked frequently at what age the iris changes to the bright

yellow of the adults. Never having kept an eagle for ob-
servations, Charlie was not sure. Two years ago he was
asked to pick up a sick eagle and take it to an island where
the game warden would feed it. The people who lived at
the place where it was being kept assured him that it was
very gentle, too weak to hurt anyone. They had fed it a
couple of rabbits and some fish that morning and said it
was certainly hungry.

Perhaps that was all that was wrong with the bird for,
when Charlie picked it up, it fought like a wild cat and he
received some nasty cuts. It was about four years old and
in a most interesting plumage. The head was partly white
and the beak was turning a bright yellow.

The iris had not attained the bright yellow of a fully
adult eagle. It was dark as yet but by another year would be
the sun color of the mature bird, the true "eagle eye."

CHAPTER EIGHTEEN

Making Friends for the Eagle

It is often hard to change a man's opinion, and this seems particularly true when it comes to reversing the belief, held for a lifetime, that because eagles and hawks are predatory they should be shot.

There are the so-called sportsmen who feel that everything that is able to move is a prospective target. They see no beauty in the graceful wheeling of a magnificent bird, high up in the sky. Their one wish seems to be to pull the trigger and cause the superb creature to fall lifeless to the ground, where it is truly useless—a bundle of feathers, no good for food and surely of doubtful value as a mounted specimen.

Very often it is not the man who owns poultry who shoots the hawk. It is the so-called, well-meaning hunter who sees the bird "bothering the chickens." Pinned down to facts, very few of the accusations made against eagles can be verified.

When Broley hears of a man living near an eyrie who is an enemy of the eagles and is known to have shot at them, he tries to make a friend of him. To threaten to prosecute him on his first interview would only tend to embitter the chap and increase his hostility towards the eagles.

Charlie calls on him frequently, talking on various subjects, omitting eagles and hawks for some time, bringing him magazines or a few cigarettes and trying to find out in what he is most interested.

After a couple of weeks he casually mentions his interest in the near-by nest and tells the man that he hopes to band the young when they are large enough. He suggests that it might be interesting for him to see and that he would be pleased to have him come along.

Usually the man is only too glad to accompany Broley and discover what this is all about. He helps carry in ladders, helps with the ropes, and so forth.

Broley talks of his hobby as they walk in, tells anecdotes about these or other pairs, and points out the rarity of having a nest so near, and how envious people are of those who are lucky enough to have one.

As a rule he makes a friend for the eagle every time, and the few who persist in their dislike will leave the birds alone for the sake of the bander, if not in fear of the heavy fine for molesting them.

While Broley does not want to overlook the serious effects of shooting bald eagles or taking their eggs, he is of the opinion that the nesting failures during the last few seasons in Florida, which might well continue, are the most serious threat at present to the status in that state.

In 1949, when sixty-five out of one hundred and eight nests went wrong, causing the non-production of some ninety-seven young birds, there was a greater loss in one season than the ninety birds reported killed in the previous ten years.

Broley believes that the solution in Florida would be the establishment of more sanctuaries or reserves such as the Everglades National Park. It was with great satisfaction that he learned this was to be enlarged.

He finds that in the South as well as in the North the police assist splendidly in the protection of the bald eagle. He was certain of this when he was arrested three times in one month while banding in Florida. People who saw him climbing up to eyries would telephone to the police that a man was robbing the nest. The chiefs of police on Florida's west coast know him now and are usually able to assure the worried informant that the "Eagle man" doesn't harm nest or birds.

Neighbors of the fine birds assist Broley in checking times of arrival and Mrs. Jean Groezinger, who lives near Bradenton, Florida, told him one November that the young birds from the nest near her home had started north that spring on the twelfth of May.

"On that day," she said, "just before leaving they sat on a dead tree not far from the house and chattered away at a great rate. I turned to my husband and told him I thought the eagles were saying goodbye to us. I remember," she went on, "he just laughed at me but we did not see them around again."

"Well, you can tell him you were right," Charlie said, "for on May fourteenth, two days later, one of these youngsters was, unfortunately, shot in North Carolina."

So far, this is the shortest lapse between an eagle's departure from the nesting site and its death that he has been able to record, but he has several instances of birds that were killed in Canada four weeks after the time he had estimated they left the nest.

A very fine nest near Bradenton, Florida, is just across Warner's Bayou from the citrus grove of Mr. and Mrs. N. M. Michaelson. They are exceedingly interested in this eyrie, especially so as they can look directly at it while eating their meals at a table near one of their large windows.

Every spring Mr. Michaelson lets Broley know if the adult birds are around, then tells him when the female begins incubating and usually, also, when the young have hatched. He likes to know a few days in advance the date on which Charlie plans to band the eaglets so that he can tell a few of his friends who might like to watch proceedings.

On the appointed day his grounds will be filled with people anxious to watch the event, most of them carrying cameras.

Mr. Michaelson, a keen observer himself, keeps the dates of the arrival in the fall, and spring leave-taking, but he has given Charlie some very interesting notes as well.

The past season there was only one young bird instead of the usual two and the Michaelsons say it was just as badly spoiled as an only child would be.

In 1950, that nest was finished up, as far as banding was concerned, by Charlie on February 25th. Mr. Michaelson wrote Charlie to say that from March 12th until the 28th the young birds practiced flying almost continuously, flapping their great wings vigorously. On the 24th they flew to the limbs just above the nest and continued to flap. They also seemed to be practicing balancing themselves.

The first flight away from the tree was made on March 29th, and Mr. Michaelson thought they were quite proud of their ability to fly.

On the afternoon and evening of April 18th, he noticed that the eaglets were making quite a commotion near the nest. They perched in trees in the vicinity, screeching incessantly. He was not sure whether they were getting ready to leave or were just hungry. At any rate he observed that the parents kept bringing food to the nest which the young promptly tore up and ate.

On May 15th, he saw them all for the last time that spring.

In the fall he noted that the pair who owned the nest returned from the north on September 9th. At any rate that was the first time he had seen them around since May. They spent some time fixing up the eyrie and the female began incubation on November 23rd. Charlie had told about the way the parents gaze proudly down at the newly hatched infant and Mr. Michaelson was delighted to see them, one on each side of the big structure, intently looking down at something in it on December 27th. He was quite sure the eggs—or egg as it turned out to be—had hatched safely.

This eaglet was banded on February 17th, 1951, with a local photographer present and some hundred and twenty-five other friends. Among them was Mr. George Patterson of Philadelphia, Mrs. Michaelson's father. Though he had a temperature of a hundred and three, he had traveled down to watch the banding.

Later Mr. Michaelson wrote to tell Charlie about the female flying in with a fish, while the eaglet, well able to fly, sat on a limb below the nest and screeched, apparently asking to have the food brought right to him. The mother paid no attention to sonny's demands but deposited the fish in the nest and sat there. Sonny kept up his querulous orders for fully four minutes before flying off the limb, out over the bayou and then up to the nest where he began tearing at the food. The mother flew away.

One of the main reasons for the banding of the American bald eagle in Florida, since at that time the bird was thought to be non-migratory, was to popularize it.

Lectures were suggested after Broley had banded a thousand eaglets or, if not lectures, at least talks to groups of people who were, or could be, interested in the emblem of the United States and in the method used by Charlie in banding them.

He had taken some pictures, both stills and movies, and he thought he could use these and also tell a little about the birds and his work.

From the first these lectures were most successful. Charlie discovered that next to banding them, he enjoyed talking about his birds. His audiences were most receptive and requests came in from many different parts of the country for such a talk.

Best of all, he found that he was not only making friends for the eagles but also for himself. He met so many charming and interesting people that he feels very grateful to his eagles for this also.

At some lectures he finds the person, male as well as female, who says, "Yes, I know it is the National Emblem but what good is it? Why should it be protected?"

These people, fortunately rare, are the same ones who would ask the monetary value of a beautiful sunset, a flower, or the starry sky. Charlie does not lose patience with them but does his best to show them his birds, as he sees them. He can be mighty convincing about them, too, and if he doesn't make a convert, at least he encourages them to be a little more friendly and a little less ready to shoot the splendid creatures.

During a lecture in Lancaster, Pennsylvania, a lady inquired, "When the eagles migrate north do they have a leader similar to the one the geese have?"

Charlie brought down the house when he said: "Madame, your National Bird would not tolerate a leader!"

CHAPTER NINETEEN

Eagles in Captivity

AN EAGLE in a cage is a sad sight. He hasn't room to fly. His feathers become bedraggled and his fierce yellow eyes, accustomed to staring into the sun from the limitless blue, lose their brilliance and become dull and lifeless when he is imprisoned.

Many lads, reading of the romantic days when hawking was the sport of kings, have stolen a young eaglet from its nest, intending to rear it like a falcon. One or two have been successful, but the training requires infinite time and patience. The eagle is a heavy bird, and to carry one around on the wrist for days at a time—the procedure necessary in training peregrines—would be exhausting.

Of course it is against the law to take these young birds, but every year one or two disappear from nests and Broley is pretty sure they have been taken by boys who hoped to train them.

Occasionally an eaglet is hurled from the nest during a windstorm. A few of these have been raised as pets but, as they require a lot of food, as well as space, they usually end up in a zoo.

In Tampa there was a very fine specimen of the bald eagle, the pet of Mr. and Mrs. W. A. Rickard, who obtained him in 1922. While still quite small this bird tumbled from a nest near Fort Myers during a hurricane. Mr. Rickard picked him up, fed, and looked after him. He had lived since then in a large cage near their home and was for years a grand, healthy creature.

Broley took him out of the cage one day to take some pictures and for awhile Jimmy, as he was called, posed nicely. He seemed to enjoy his perch, a moss-draped crossbar. Then, deciding he had had enough, he flew off and away, going about two blocks before settling down on a curb.

Broley found him after a brief search and, taking him by his huge wings, walked him back to the cage. He protested a bit but did not try to attack them. That was his last outing and he seemed content to stay in the cage. He was quite fond of being petted and would rub against the Rickards affectionately when they went into the cage, begging to have his head scratched.

He made a good watch-dog also, for his staccato cry rang out whenever strangers came around. Admirers brought fish and wild animals that had been killed to him, and Broley, when he found an eyrie with a great many fish, would often take one or two back for Jimmy. Fresh water was kept in the cage always and the eagle liked to wash his talons off after he had torn up his food. At a suggestion from Mr. Rickard that his feet were dirty he would hop over to the pan and rinse off first one then the other big yellow claw.

Two years ago Jimmy proved that it was misnamed for after twenty-eight years of captivity she laid an egg! Two more were laid afterwards but the name was not changed. The eggs caused a great deal of discussion but, as it is not unusual for parrots kept for years in a cage to do this, it was thought that the eggs might be a sign that the reproductive cycle was nearly over. Last summer Mr. Rickard's foot became infected, and it was found necessary to amputate it. While he was in the hospital, Jimmy moped about and seemed to miss him. Another egg was laid at this time. Mr. Rickard returned to his home but did not recover, as was hoped, and passed away. A day after his death friends went out to feed Jimmy and found the eagle dead on the floor of his cage beside the egg. Did he die of grief? Eagles have lived in zoos for forty years. Possibly in the wild they might live much longer. A hundred years has been suggested as the length of their lifetime. It is hard to know. Broley is hoping that, years from now, some of his banded birds will give the answer.

An eagle wearing band number 44/812985 was banded near Sarasota on January 22nd, 1948, when it was four weeks old. Broley remembers how uncomfortable his climb was on that occasion. He must have stepped on an ants' nest when making his connections for, when he was about half way up to the nest, the insects began biting him. There was nothing he could do except hang with one hand from time to time and scratch while his audience on the ground, a number of them women, made amused comments.

Up in the big nest, which contained eighteen air plants, he managed to crouch down, out of sight, so that he could rid himself of a few of the little pests before he banded the bird.

In October of that year the eaglet was found near Pittsburg, Pennsylvania, with a broken wing. At first the lad who found it had the bird in his home. It became very tame and would run to anyone of the family for food. Then it began running after visitors also, and they, fearing this ferocious looking creature, scrambled out of its way as quickly as possible. This seemed to amuse the bird and it chased everyone. The family decided it might hurt a child or even a grown-up and it was taken to the very fine zoo there and placed in a large, roomy cage with two golden eagles.

In April of the next year Broley visited it there and held it while a news photographer took some pictures. The bird was in fine condition, except for the top of one wing which had had to be cut off. Broley asked the caretaker if the larger golden eagles abused this crippled bald eagle.

"No sir," he answered most emphatically, "Baldie rules the roost. When we put food in there, the golden eagles don't dare come near it until this chap has had all he wants."

It is my husband's belief that if this bird ever managed to get free and then mated, it would attack anyone nearing its nest. Since it has become acquainted with people and has found that it can frighten them away, it would enjoy doing so.

One year Broley found, in a nest on Pine Island, near Fort Myers, a good-sized eaglet and another only about five days old. He knew he would not be down that way again; so, after banding the large bird, he decided to try to tag the smaller one also. He wrapped the band well with paper string which was being tried out at that time. He did not know whether or not this would work but thought he would chance it.

A year later he went in to visit the very fine zoo belonging to Bill Piper at Bonita Springs. "I have a fine young eagle here," Mr. Piper said, "picked up injured at Lake Okeechobee. It's got a band on, maybe one of yours."

Charlie went over to see it. It was one of his bands, and by checking he discovered that this was the eaglet on which he had put the band stuffed with paper string. He was glad to see that the band fitted nicely. He had known that the string, after a good wetting, would disintegrate but was not too sure this would not happen before the talon was large enough to retain the band. The bird was in splendid condition, except for the injured wing, and he was able to check its plumage from time to time.

Mr. Piper was telling him about four skunks which had been brought in to him by a friend. He kept the cute little fellows for about two weeks then, deciding that he did not want them in the zoo, put them in a box and took them out to a wood lot he owned about four miles away. Two days later he had to go back again and there were the four little fellows sitting forlornly atop the box; they didn't know where to go.

Mrs. H. R. Mills of St. Petersburg told Charlie about a little skunk that visited her home last winter. She fed it and kept it overnight in the house during a spell of chilly weather, leaving the door partly open so that it could come and go. One night she was wakened by something soft pressing up against her throat. The little skunk had gotten into her bed and was cuddling up to her for warmth!

CHAPTER TWENTY

Egg Collectors

WHEN HE first began his banding operations in Florida, Broley found that egg collectors were very active there. At that time a set—two—of bald eagle eggs brought ten dollars. He was told of a man over near Merritt Island on the east coast who had collected a bushel basket of them.

In Tampa he discovered one man who had a Federal permit to collect them. Fortunately, he did not have a State license so after much time and trouble, Broley was able to have his activities in this line stopped. On many of the trees he had nailed cleats, planning to rob them every spring.

Many of these collectors claim that the bald eagle will lay a second clutch, or even a third, if the first set is taken. Broley is positive that this assumption is erroneous but is willing to concede that there might be a rare exception. He has never known it to happen in any of his nests.

Smaller birds will lay again and again. A yellow-shafted woodpecker, or flicker, laid a total of fifty-three eggs when, during that period, the newly laid egg was removed each day. Yellow warblers have been known to cover up their own eggs with one or more that a cowbird sneaked into their tiny basket. We have one such nest with four

tiers, showing how hard the tiny bird had worked to out-
wit that parasite.

In Broley's experience, once the eggs of the eagle have
been taken, the bird makes no further attempt that season
to raise a brood. It may build a new nest but will not lay
that year.

William Leon Dawson, who did much research work
on the eagles of California, was positive that if the eggs
were destroyed or taken away the birds would not nest
again until the following year.

In Ontario, the eggs are seldom taken, so Broley has no
data as to that. However in early spring when the eggs are
first laid in the eyries there, muskrat trappers or woodcut-
ters often keep the big birds off the eggs inadvertently.
Some do not realize there is an eagle's nest in the vicinity. In
such cases, when the egg has been so chilled that the embryo is killed, the eagle will continue to sit for a time, then
will stay around the nest, but flies off when anyone ap-
proaches. Broley can always tell if this has happened. An
eagle with eggs will leave the nest when disturbed, but flies
around, right overhead, giving her warning cry and swooping at the intruder. When the nest is empty, or the eggs are
infertile, she goes right away and does not return until after
the person leaves.

If they laid a second set, there would certainly be no
reason why she should not do so if she found her first lot
did not hatch. In Florida, Broley has found an infertile egg
buried deeply under the mossy lining, but in that case no
third one had been laid. He has watched the adults at nests
where the eggs were always infertile and after the time for

hatching has passed, the birds incubated very sporadically, as though they knew well it was useless.

While he does not like to say so, he believes that the former large population of southern bald eagles over in the district around Merritt Island has decreased in number because of the egg collecting that was so prevalent there.

His opinion is that these larger birds cannot lay eggs at irregular times, that a great deal of physical preparation is made for this event. This is also the belief of Doctor F. B. Hutt, Professor of Poultry Genetics at Cornell.

At this time there is no need, in Broley's judgment, for any further permits being granted for the purpose of collecting eggs. Museums and colleges have large cases of them which are available for study. Our birds are growing fewer in number, and if we want to keep all our species we must guard against loss, even in the interest of science. Charlie realizes that there are certain facts which he could determine, such as the fertility or lack of it in his nester's eggs, but he does not want to test these lest there be a loss of good eggs.

In our time, such birds as the wild pigeon, the heath hen and the Labrador duck have vanished and our whooping cranes are going. Care and watchfulness are keeping our Hudsonian godwits, the trumpeter swans, and a few other species. Certainly we do not want to see the bald eagle, the national emblem of a mighty nation, wiped from this continent because some greedy men want to make a little easy money.

CHAPTER TWENTY-ONE

Photographing Eagles

To DATE, practically no good movies in color have been taken of adult eagles feeding young except the ones that Broley has gotten in the last couple of years. It is a simple matter to build a blind on the ground and very easy to slip into it without the parents catching sight of you even if they are flying about in the vicinity. It is quite another matter entirely to try and get up into a blind, sixty or seventy feet from the ground, and evade the keen eyes of the king of birds. Yet to obtain really good pictures the photographer must be somewhat higher than the nest and not over forty feet from it.

This means a suitable tree must be growing near the nest tree, and it must be on the southwest side of the nest in order to have the sun behind the camera.

The nest must not be shaded, as it is in the majority of eagle trees; and even when all these requirements have been met, the photographer, when using kodachrome, is still at the mercy of the weather. Perhaps it clouds over before the eagle comes to the nest to feed the young, or again, the light may be perfect but a strong wind has sprung up, which not only sways the nest but also rocks the blind back and forth, certainly not assisting in the taking of good shots.

In comparing notes with Dr. A. A. Allen, Dr. Charles Proctor, and others who have spent hours in blinds waiting for an eagle to return to the eyrie, they all agree that it is one of the most wary of birds about coming back, once it has discovered people in the vicinity.

When the chance to get into the blind without one eagle seeing you comes, the other, left on guard quickly gives the alarm to the returning mate, which immediately veers off and avoids coming in. The photographer can be certain that he will have a six-hour wait before she returns.

The birds go off fishing or hunting, but even when successful do not come back until they feel sure that a long enough time has elapsed so that the intruder will have become disheartened and left.

Broley has put up four different blinds, but in only one did everything break in his favor so that he was able to take about three hundred feet of really good pictures of the parents feeding the young.

Two days spent in the first blind, from seven in the morning until four-thirty in the afternoon, produced nothing. The adults refused to come near the nest. Perhaps the blind, constructed of chicken wire with dark green awning material inside, was not sufficiently covered with palm fronds, which had been worked into the wire. He took a lot of pictures of the young and later obtained some good ones when they were practicing flying, but by that time they were able to tear up their own food and the parents did not remain long at the nest.

The second blind was also discouraging. After many

hours spent in building it, the day was set for getting some pictures. Broley went to it well before daylight but had no luck. Next day he did manage to get a few shots but the bird seemed wary, afraid.

Returning two days later, he discovered that some vandal had shot both young birds; they were dead in the nest. All his hard work, as well as the eagle's, had been spoiled by this sadistic act.

The third blind produced most satisfactory results during the first two days, when the young were a month old. He got some excellent pictures. Returning four weeks later to complete the story, showing the young well grown, another tragedy was discovered. The young were gone! They were too small to fly and the question of what happened has not as yet been answered.

CHAPTER TWENTY-TWO

Future Outlook for the Bald Eagle

WHEN CHARLES BROLEY began banding operations in Florida in 1939, he estimated that in many areas there was an eagle's nest every mile along the west coast. For some years these continued to be active and one young bird, at least, was raised each year. Now, so many of these trees have been cut, leaving no suitable ones near by, that of his one hundred and twenty-five nests he has only about ninety left.

True, he has found a few new nests. Many of the birds have retreated to the cypress swamps where there are suitable trees, but these, too, are in danger; so much land is being cleared for vegetable gardens, groves, or for building purposes, that there will soon be no trees left, large enough to hold a heavy nest.

Florida seems to have entered a cycle of hot, dry winters, which are very hard on eggs and small young. If the weather is too warm, many of the eggs do not hatch, due to lack of moisture to facilitate incubation. The winter of 1950 was quite cool, but the hurricane in the autumn had upset the big birds and for this reason few young were hatched.

During the war years, and for some time afterwards, it was difficult to buy guns, shells, and so forth. Now they are plentiful again, and the result can be seen in the number of young eagles that are shot.

The five-hundred-dollar fine does not stop a number of these sharpshooters who say they think that the large, dark young one is a hawk. True, this is no excuse, for they should not shoot hawks either, but they are usually allowed to go with a reprimand. Most of the bands sent in are said to have been taken off a bird "picked up dead." The Fish and Wild Life Service have no means of proving that this is not so and must, perforce, accept the statement.

From 1939 to 1946, Broley says he saw little change in the nesting success of eagles in Florida. Every year the pairs he was watching brought forth broods of one or two young with a usual nesting mortality of about thirty per cent. The year 1945 was an exception—the hurricane the previous October badly disrupted nesting; 1949 was a disastrous year and the years since have been worse.

In 1947, out of one hundred and twenty-three nests under observation, fifty-one produced no young, a failure of forty-one per cent. During 1948, Charlie was watching a hundred and twenty-five nests but in only sixty-five of them did young develop successfully.

By 1949, he had lost a number of nests and so had only one hundred and eight to check. Sixty-five of these produced no young, a failure of sixty per cent. He had been watching these eyries carefully so knew pretty well what had caused the failures.

Pairs returned to twenty-three of these nests, but no eggs were laid. They did a lot of repairing from time to time and sat around in or near the nest but would fly right away when anyone came near, showing no anxiety at all. Often mated pairs will use a nest for a feeding station, both bringing in the food which they share.

Sometimes, for no apparent reason, a pair of eagles will, as it were, declare a sabbatical. They just don't raise a brood. Nothing has happened to the nest and they may fuss around, adding sticks, moss, or even bright gewgaws to it, but no eggs are laid.

Although eggs were deposited in thirty-one eyries that year, none of them hatched. Possibly the very dry weather was to blame or the birds were kept off at a crucial time; whatever the cause, no young hatched.

The adults did not return to four of the nests. One of the pair might have been killed or they might have grown too old to reproduce. They will leave a nest if the eggs or young have been taken, or if the young birds die; either may have been the reason.

Great horned owls usurped three nests, and the trees which had held three others were felled. Boys robbed one nest of its two eggs.

In the eastern United States there are two definite nesting concentrations of the bald eagle; the Chesapeake Bay region of Maryland, and the State of Florida. Some of the other states have a few pair still but, as a rule, these build in remote, inaccessible spots, away from gunners or would-be falconers. It should be the ambition of every state, of every district really, to have a pair of these fine birds, emblematic of their country, living near by, where they may be seen in all their grandeur, in all their graceful strength and imperial beauty. What if we do lose a few grouse, a few ducks to them! Why should we reserve the rights to all these things for ourselves? For my part, I gladly give all my share in any game, in any fish even, to the eagles.

We are willing to spend thousands, after a species has become extinct, or nearly so, to try and bring it back. Why not spend a little now to keep our eagles here? It was their country first!

Alaska has had a wonderful population of eagles of the northern or *Alascanus* type. Alas, *had* is the word, for, at the rate they are being shot for the bounty, the bird will be wiped out there unless something is done about it, and soon.

This eagle has been accused of killing salmon, of preying on foxes in fur farms, and on the sooty grouse. It was on account of his depredations on salmon going up the river to spawn that the bounty was first put on this glorious bird. At that time it was fifty cents. Later it was increased to a dollar; then two years ago the government offered to pay two dollars to everyone bringing in the talons of this bird. And this was to people living under the flag of the United States of America who recognize the eagle as the emblem of their country!

One of the attractions of the beautiful inside passage from Victoria, British Columbia, northward was the many bald eagles to be seen, perched in trees along the shore, their snow-white heads contrasting so brilliantly with the dark green of the background. Now there are few to be seen, although in 1922 Major Allan Brooks thought that with so many winding inlets and channels, and so much uninhabited land, there was still a tremendous area for the nesting of the great birds. He mentioned that he had often seen forty or more together, but that was very likely at a spot where the salmon, after spawning, had died and the eagles had collected to feed.

A very well known authority on Alaska has said, "It is a disgrace to have a bounty on the bald eagle. True, it does provide some money to pay for ammunition that a certain element loves to expend in shooting at anything alive." The number of eagles now present in Alaska could do no conceivable harm to any economic interest. The charge against them that they eat salmon is true but it is ridiculous to assume that the limited number of eagles along the coastal streams of Alaska have had any effect upon the hordes of salmon that migrate into the streams in good years. Netting and illegal trolling are the primary causes of any depletion and, of course, the use of the fish for canning.

In all the studies of predation that have been carried on so extensively lately by conservationists, it is clearly shown that predators do not destroy, or even noticeably cut down, the population of the creatures upon which they feed. They change their habits whenever it is necessary and live on the food that is most abundant and most easily caught. If not preyed upon this abundant prey would be wiped out by diseases or starvation anyway, or their numbers would be cut down by internecine feuds.

In 1941 the Fish and Wildlife Service undertook an

analysis of the stomachs of three hundred and four bald eagles. Seventy-seven per cent of the food was fish, with salmon making up twenty-three and a half per cent, herring three and a half per cent, and coarse fish of no economic value making up the other fifty.

Now most of this salmon is carrion; fish that died after spawning. A further piece of research proved that out of all the eggs laid by the red salmon only about one per cent of the hatched young reach the sea and seventy-nine per cent of these are lost before ever returning to spawn.

Waterfowl made up fifteen and a half per cent of the food with ducks, mostly scoters taken along the coast, predominating. Only two point eight per cent were mammals, and one point one per cent of deer remains was found, and this was carrion.

It is a well-known fact that the young in fur farms where there is overcrowding contract many diseases. Numbers of them die and these are put out by the owners of such ranches to attract eagles. The rancher lies in wait until the eagles come in to feed, then shoots them for the two-dollar bounty, adding insult to injury by claiming that the birds were "feeding on my foxes." He doesn't say that the foxes were dead. Anyhow he is repaid, as he thinks, for his loss of the pelts.

During the eighteen years from 1903 to 1922 bounties at the rate of fifty cents were paid on fifteen thousand and more eagles. From 1923 until 1940, when it had been increased to a dollar, sixty-three thousand, six hundred and ninety-six were brought in. In 1949, the fee was raised to two dollars and in that one year seven thousand, four hundred and fifty-five people were paid for making an appalling total of eighty-six thousand, eight hundred and ninety-six splendid birds shot down from greed.

The total, at the present time of writing is, I believe, one hundred and fourteen thousand, two hundred and ninety-one birds, so that Alaska has paid out more than a hundred thousand dollars to people who shot down, cruelly and needlessly, the emblem of a great country. And to what purpose?

We would do far better to pay the fisheries, the fur farmers, and others NOT to shoot our eagles than to permit them to destroy the majestic presence of the emperor of the air. Should one industry or two make a profit at the esthetic expense of all the rest of us?

While some may argue that the eagle has little economic value—I do not agree with this—it certainly has a great attraction value. This is apparent by the number of people who come to us, or write to us, to ask where and when they can catch sight of one. Tourists in Florida have said to us, "My trip will be a success if I can see just one eagle."

Recently Broley received a number of letters from people who thought he ought to go up and try to save the Alaskan eagles. "They really need you," they wrote.

In the eastern United States there are still some bald eagles and they are well protected and these people who love their birds were justly outraged when the three bills before Congress last year to extend Federal protection to the harried Alaskan eagle were thrown out. Men are always ready to blame something else for their own misdeeds, but it is illegal netting, and not the eagles, which is depleting the salmon.

On Pine Island, near Fort Myers, Broley in 1942 found twelve active eagle nests. These were in a tract of land one and a half miles wide and six miles in length—about nine square miles of pine forest. By January 1949, practically all the large timber had been cut and only four occupied nests could be found. There were many adult eagles around but they were not nesting, apparently. Yet they did not want to leave this territory which they liked; or, perhaps, not having found a suitable tree, they were taking a year's vacation.

From the first thousand eagles banded in Florida Broley has had ninety recoveries, which means that nine per cent of his eaglets have met disaster, since almost every band returned is from the leg of a dead eagle, banded while active and healthy in the nest.

Returns have come from almost every state east of the Mississippi and from Canadian provinces as far west as Manitoba.

Dr. Herbert R. Mills, who is an ardent and well-known conservationist of Florida, helped Broley make an estimate of the number of eyries in that southern state a couple of years ago. They put the number at four hundred and fifty. So many are being lost each year that they believe another ten years will see few suitable sites left for these adult eagles. Where will the newer generations build?

Many of the first thousand he banded should already be nesting, and their parents as well. There is still some good timber in Georgia and the Carolinas, but will these birds go there? Broley is doubtful, especially in the case of the older eagles, who do not like to leave a chosen region.

In eastern Ontario the bald eagle seems to be holding its ground fairly well. There is still an abundance of big timber up there and should be for years to come.

In a radius of twenty miles from our island home in Ontario, Canada, behind the Thousand Islands, there are fifteen nests. There has been little change in the number in the past forty years.

It is rather interesting, and I did not think it prophetic, that one of the plans Charlie had made for our honeymoon twenty-eight years ago, was to show me an eagle's nest. The tree in which this was situated was on the lake where, for the first time, I had come to spend some time at the cottage which has ever since been our home for the summer months.

I remember my amazement at the size of the big eyrie, the first one I had ever seen. There were no birds around it, but it was the beginning of August and Charlie thinks these eagles also go further north in summer, coming back in the fall. We were told the nest had been used that spring; that the two fine young ones had flown away safely.

Charlie had planned to buy the tree, to make sure it would not be cut down, but the owner told him that was not necessary. "As long as I own this farm they'll be welcome to that tree and the land around it. They are safe here and I do not plan to sell this farm."

A few years ago the birds moved to a new site nearer the water and, as it also is on land belonging to this neighbor, we do not worry about them losing their nesting tree.

Sometimes this splendid nest had three young ones. Charlie says he finds young more numerous in his northern nests, the northern eagles being more prolific and seeming to have more luck in their eggs hatching. The young are not nearly so pugnacious, nor do they quarrel with each other so much.

Charlie has now banded one thousand one hundred and eighty-five eaglets. He hopes to continue for years to come, although he is now past seventy. People who see him climb so easily and lithely up a tree find it hard to believe that he can be that age.

A number of experiments have been suggested to him and perhaps some day he may try some of them out. For instance, he has three nests in which the eggs have never hatched. Someone asked him why he did not change one of these eggs for one from a nest where both hatch regularly.

Too, the question of what an eagle can carry is always a matter of interest. Possibly he could make some tests with weights and get some data on this.

As he says, it is a grand thing that Nature doesn't show you all her secrets at once. She is generous though, to all who love her and her children of the wild. Broley believes he will find new facets of study in his beloved eagle for the rest of his life, even if he does have to stop climbing trees at some future date.

It is certainly true that if he cannot band them, he can at least talk about them, and he enjoys this also.

CHAPTER TWENTY-THREE

The 1951 and 1952 Seasons in Florida

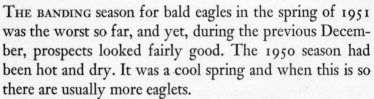

THE BANDING season for bald eagles in the spring of 1951 was the worst so far, and yet, during the previous December, prospects looked fairly good. The 1950 season had been hot and dry. It was a cool spring and when this is so there are usually more eaglets.

In November, 1950, when he made his first survey for the ensuing season, Charlie found that many of his nests had been rebuilt. Some nesting trees had been cut down; owls had taken over a few eyries. At one nest something new had been added. A drive-in movie theatre had been constructed near Sarasota, and about two hundred feet behind its parking lot there was one of his large nests. There were generally two fine, scrappy eaglets in this. Charlie chuckled away, talking of the picture he planned to take in which he hoped to show the young birds on the nest watching the flicker of a picture on the big screen in front of them.

Unfortunately, when he went back four weeks later to check, he discovered that, like those in a number of his other nests, the eggs had not hatched. This was the first time in his experience that anything had upset the nesting at this tree. He did not think the activity around the drive-in had been the cause for the parents had hung around all the time the land was being cleared, and the building was going on.

Incidentally, the owner of this drive-in, who was very interested in the nest, told Charlie that the land was swarming with rattlesnakes when they began clearing it. He said the big bulldozer would come in festooned with them after it had been used in grubbing out roots, trees, and brush. He was hoping the eagles would attend to any strays left around. Charlie had always been careful in this area as it was one he recognized as attractive to snakes; he had always scrutinized the ground carefully when working there.

There were a number of pairs of eagles around which, instead of settling down to the business of raising a brood, seemed satisfied to hang around near the water, apparently just loafing. In some cases they repaired their nests, adding new branches, fresh grass, and Spanish moss to them. But they would fly right away, as if unconcerned, when anyone approached.

Through January and February his banding trips continued to be unsuccessful. He would depart with the intention of staying six or seven days in the field but would return in three, sometimes only two, to say there just weren't any more eaglets to band. He would have tagged those in the two or three nests that were ready and be unable to find any more old enough.

In many cases the eggs did not hatch at all although the

birds incubated as usual. The previous season the nests were very dry. Usually when he climbs to one of these structures and bands the young, he spends some time examining the debris. The eagle, as was said, carried queer objects up to his castle, but that is not his only reason for searching about. It is possible to tell on what the adult or young have been feeding by the material left in the nest. Broley's findings go far to refute the tales of those people who picture the big birds as living solely on poultry or on song and game birds.

In most seasons the nests would be decidedly moist when he pulled up the top lining; last season's dust would rise when he moved sticks or lining about. Most of us know that eggs require a certain amount of moisture if the chicks are to hatch properly. In dry weather, poultry eggs are often sprinkled, sometimes even immersed in water for a few minutes. This serves a double purpose, for a fertile egg may be told from an infertile one or a fresh one that has been laid after the hen had brooded for awhile.

Broley had in all ninety-two nests under observation in 1951. Normally he should have had at least a hundred eaglets from these but the net result was twenty-five birds.

Thirty of the nests were not used at all, a potential loss of forty young. A pair will take a season off now and then but never will so many be idle in a single year unless there is some other reason. The eggs did not hatch in nineteen nests which he had checked and marked as containing the precious ovals at the usual time.

He was puzzled as to the reason for all this. It had been a cool season all through, which favored good incubation

as compared with the abnormally hot weather of the previous year. Then he was told about a vicious hurricane
which hurtled through in mid-October. This was what
had disrupted the laying of the eggs. As mentioned elsewhere, such a storm is very hard on eagles, coming as it
does just at the time that they are ready to eject their eggs.
Eagles are apparently of a very nervous temperament.

The terrific storm in November along the Atlantic coast
had upset the eagles nesting around the Chesapeake Bay
area.

Four of the trees which contained eyries were cut down.
He found nests which could have been new ones built by
the routed pair, but they were empty. Quite likely they had
worked at rebuilding but realized it was too late to raise a
brood that season, or the female might have been one of
the early-nesting type and had simply resorbed her eggs.

Owls managed to take possession of seven of the eyries.
Eagles do not see as well as owls at night and Charlie thinks
it is at that time the fights for possession take place. He has
heard hooting and the eagles' screaming at night when he
slept in the vicinity of a nest.

The hardest jolt of all was the complete disappearance
of the young from three nests. They were too small to
have been taken by boys yearning to train them as falcons;
besides the nests were too high for anyone to climb who
was not equipped with ladders. There were no marks of
climbing irons, and no cleats had been nailed to the trees. It
was certainly an unpleasant and tragic mystery.

Wildcats are said to be able to get up after young birds
in trees but it did seem an arduous task even for a lithe, big

cat. Surely it could obtain food much more easily on the ground. I suggested that someone in a helicopter could have taken them but I'm sure this did not happen.

Summing it all up, Charlie discovered that out of his ninety-two nests he banded birds in only nineteen. Four young ones got away from their homes when he climbed up; he had left them too long, or had, in two cases, located the nests for the first time when the young were fully grown and, though he ascended at once, the bird went off just as he reached the top and, being able to fly well, kept right on out of sight.

Of the nineteen nests where he banded, only six held two birds. In the others the eagle had laid only one egg, or else the second was infertile, or something had killed the embryo in the shell.

His loss then was seventy-seven per cent, the highest yet. The year 1946 was his banner year. He put bracelets on one hundred and fifty eaglets that spring, the eighth year of his work. Many of the trees had been visited and the young tagged each year. A great many were banded for the sixth or seventh time, showing very clearly that banding does not bother the eagles at all.

In 1947, he banded one hundred and thirteen birds from one hundred and twenty-three eyries, a loss of forty-two per cent. His total for 1948 was eighty-five birds, and this fifty-one per cent loss worried him greatly, but he had put the blame largely on hot weather and strong winds.

In 1949, when, out of his one hundred and eight nests, he tagged only sixty birds, he was alarmed. Then the next years' totals were only twenty-five each.

This should be a warning for everyone. If the weather can cause this drastic reduction in numbers we must guard more zealously than ever against all man-caused losses. Surely no one wants the American bald eagle, the national emblem of the United States, to join the list—already too long—of birds that are extinct.

William Leon Dawson has said, "The passing of the bald eagle is doubtless ordained by the same factors, bravado, recklessness, and revenge, which have decreed the destruction of his golden kinsman." Men seemingly cannot endure the presence of any large bird without trying to shoot it. As an alibi he is ready to claim that it takes fowl, pigs, lambs, or even babies.

Garden clubs, bird clubs, and bird lovers generally, might look into the possibility of buying an eagle's nesting tree with enough land about to protect the pair. We know of one gentleman in Florida who is planning to put up a sort of platform in a large tree on his property in the hope that an eagle will use it as a foundation for a nest. Fish hawks used to be induced to build near certain localities by putting up old wheels; maybe the eagle could be coaxed back also.

Shooting, or interfering with an eagle, or taking eggs or young, should be punished much more severely than it is.

A group of returns which reached him recently have added to Broley's worry about his eagles. In the list he found the number of an eagle banded on January 28th, 1947, at Englewood, Florida, which had been shot at Huntington, Pennsylvania, by a Mrs. Joseph McCall, on August 26th, 1949.

In her letter replying to his request for an explanation, Mrs. McCall said she had shot the bird because it had made three trips to her hen yard and killed fifty laying hens, valued at two dollars and fifty cents each.

The eagle is not a killer like the weasel or the great horned owl which kill for love of it. The eagle goes after his food, kills it, eats it, and that is that. He might return to the same place again but would not kill until he was ready to eat the food. He doesn't leave carcasses about.

Charlie wrote to Mrs. McCall to ask her if she had seen the eagle kill any of the poultry and how often she had seen it about. She answered that she hadn't seen it kill the hens but they were dead and the only time she saw the eagle at the hen yard was the time she shot it.

Another state has been added to the list[1] of those in which his eagles have been found. A young bird banded in St. Petersburg, Florida, on February 9th, 1949, was picked up north of Mora, Minnesota, on May 17th, 1949, marking the farthest west that he has known his eaglets to fly.

Disaster overtook a touring eaglet in June of 1948. Banded in Englewood, Florida, on February 25th, 1948, it flew into a high tension wire whilst looking over New Brunswick, Canada.

There were three other returns besides the ones listed, one of them a Canadian eagle Charlie had banded near his summer home in Ontario on June 6th, 1949. It was found dead in October of the same year, about a hundred miles west of its birthplace.

[1] See Appendix for chart of recoveries.

He dreads to think of getting returns for the few birds banded in 1950 and 1951. He hopes there will be no more hurricanes or hot, dry winters in Florida. At any rate, he is sure that it would be impossible for him to band another thousand eagles, even if he were ten years younger, unless as has been suggested, he should travel to Alaska and put bracelets on the young ones left up there.

But news of his young eagles is not always tragic. Here in his own words is the story of what he calls a "happy incident."

"I am not too anxious to hear about many of the eaglets I band since it usually means that the bird has met disaster through striking a high-tension wire, being caught in a fox trap or, worst of all, has been shot by some thoughtless gunner.

"In November of 1941, while we were in Tampa, Florida, I read in a Canadian paper that an eagle wearing band number 34/709962 had been picked up by the police of Picton, Ontario, with an injured wing. They thought it might have come in contact with a plane. The eagle had been placed in a large cage on the main street with a sign propped near by asking passers-by to drop coins in a box as a contribution to the Red Cross.

"The newspaper article further stated that the bird was to be sent over to Timber Island in Lake Ontario, where there were other eagles which would, of course, feed the injured one. I knew they would do no such thing.

"Checking the band number, I found that this was one of my birds. I had banded it near Delta, Ontario, on July

3rd, 1940—a year and four months previously. Picton is about seventy-five miles from Delta.

"I was worried about an eagle with a bad wing being placed on an island, especially in the winter, and I wrote to the Chief of Police at Picton asking in what condition the bird was. I did not receive a reply.

"Two years later Timber Island was given to Queen's University of Kingston, Ontario. One of the professors called me up one day to tell me that he was going over to the island the following day and to ask me if I would not like to go along. He had been told there was an eagle's nest on it and he thought I might like to band the young.

"About noon the next day we arrived on the north shore of Lake Ontario and went to get a boat from a fisherman; the island was about a mile out.

"The man asked me what I was going to do with all the ropes and ladders we were piling in the boat and I told him I planned to climb to an eagle's nest.

" 'Say,' he began, 'about two years ago the police from Picton brought me an eagle with an injured wing and asked me to take it over to Timber Island. It had a band on too, but I forget the number.'

"Well, did you?" I asked for the professor and I realized this was the eagle I had worried about.

" 'I was very busy just then,' he said, 'so I let the bird go in the yard and fed it all the fish it could eat. How that bird could finish them off! In a few days it became quite friendly and would follow me around in the mornings until I tossed it some food. After about three weeks an eagle flew over the house towards Timber Island and my bird made a running take-off down that path and flew right over to the island with the first one.'

"That's the kind of recovery I like to get."

Young eagles have been shot, found dead, or picked up wounded in Florida during the months of January, February, March, April, May, and June. There are no reports in that state for July, August, or September; but one was taken in October, two in November, and three in December.

In Georgia, none has been recovered in January, February, or March. Two have been found in April, three in May, and one in June. There were none at all during August or September, but one is recorded for October, and another in November.

Arkansas had a return in May, and one eaglet was shot in Mississippi in July. South Carolina reported one in April and another in May, three in June, one in July, and two in August. They also had quite a late recovery of one in December. He must have enjoyed the north.

North Carolina's total of six birds were all in May, except for one that stayed until June. Kentucky had one in May. Virginia had two in April and two more in May.

Pennsylvania had its earliest in May, another in June, two in July, and four in August, making eight returns for that state. This is most surprising, for that is one state where game laws and migratory rulings are very rigorously enforced and it is surprising that so many bald eagles should have been shot in the spring. Of course these were youngsters and all dark in plumage; they may have been thought to be large hawks.

Indiana's lone report is for July, and Illinois reported one in July and another in August. The eaglet reported in May from Massachusetts left Florida very soon after taking off from the eyrie, and so did the one shot in Connecticut in April.

New York had three recoveries in May, and Michigan one. Birds were shot in Maine in May and August, and the one that made the long flight to the west, only to be shot in Mora, Minnesota, was there by May.

The Canadian records show that the birds lost little time getting up there. Quebec and New Brunswick report them in May. They were around, of course, in June, July, August, and September, but no Florida eagles have been recovered there later than that month.

Nova Scotia sent in data on eagles taken in June, September, and one in October. Prince Edward Island had one to report in June.

The most northerly flight so far reported is to an island on Lake Winnipeg in Manitoba. This young adventurer traveled about twenty-five hundred miles from his home site and then was captured when he investigated a wolf trap on the twenty-fifth of July. He had been banded at Placida, Florida, on February 26th of that year, 1947.

We sometimes speak of a family as being unlucky. Tragedies happen to them that neighbors are spared. Charlie has two nests in Florida that are definitely unlucky. So far, every bird banded in them has been shot, not in Florida, but after the young move north. In spite of all the parents' care and the long weeks they have spent rearing the young, they have no progeny to carry on their line.

Oddly enough neither nest is very near habitations. Charlie thinks birds brought up in eyries near a house become too used to people and are not wary enough. We can only say that these nests are ill starred.

Here is the list of returns he has had from bald eagles banded in Leeds County, Ontario, about eighty miles west of Ottawa.

Number	Place	Banded	Found	Date
34-709962	Delta	3 July '40	Picton	13 Nov. '41
40-810069	Delta	9 June '41	Kent, Md.	22 Dec. '41
40-810067	Delta	9 June '41	Delta	10 Oct. '41
41-807429	Portland	23 June '42	Pennsylvania	17 Oct. '42
41-812210	Portland	18 June '43	Tennessee	12 Dec. '43
42-800679	Portland	24 June '45	Alabama	14 Nov. '45
44-812977	Anglins Farm Delta	17 June '47	Oswego. N. Y.	14 Sept. '47
45-802166	Portland	6 June '49	Bowmanville, Ontario	26 Oct. '49
42-800675	Charleston	22 June '45	Lake James, N. C.	4 July '49

Four of these birds were reported "found dead." Two were discovered injured; one was later released and the other three were simply reported "shot."

The one that was found dead in North Carolina on July fourth had gone south much earlier than they usually do. And what a thing to happen to it on that day!

While Charlie dreads receiving returns of his eagles, for in almost every case it means the bird has been killed, he enjoys checking the flights. Although his Canadian birds fly south for the winter they seem to take a trip northward when they first leave their tree-top castles. At any rate through August and September he does not see any eagles around the lakes where he bands in May and June. Then in late September or early October they will be flying around again, riding the air waves on a windy day, fishing from the rocks near the creek or sitting perched on their lookout trees. The eagle spends a lot of time just gazing over its domain, and who can blame it—especially in the glorious northern fall weather?

The 1952 Season in Florida

The season of 1952 has been most disappointing in the regular banding area but numerous reports have come in from other parts telling of successful nestings. Alex Sprunt writes of eight nests with young to be seen in the Okee-chobee region. Steven F. Briggs of Naples and Milwaukee sent word that he had seen a number of occupied nests in the mangroves along the Florida Keys and many others, even from as far away as Washington, have been anxious to have Broley band eaglets in their vicinity. Unfortunately, since his time is limited this spring, Broley will not attempt to go to these, much as he would like to. He plans to stay later next year and try to cover a larger area.

Many of the nests that looked promising in December had to be written off later on. In several cases he knew that the incubating birds had been kept off by activity on the ground below the eyries. So much land is being reclaimed or dredged up from the bays that, as eagles prefer to have their tree-top homes near the water, the big machines which are being used to pump up the sand very often keep them alerted through the daylight hours and the eggs spoil.

In 1952, more people arrived in Florida than ever before. Trees were cut, areas were cleared out, new highways were built, as well as hundreds of motels and houses. No wonder the eagles moved back into the cypress swamps or onto the Keys or even decided not to nest at all. As one resident of Florida remarked—"There are just too many people to leave room for eagles also."

Possibly the rush of tourists to the West Coast has driven the eagles inland and that is why we hear of more successful nesting in the central part of Florida. As previously mentioned, reports from some fourteen nests around the Okeechobee and Everglades National Park region brought the welcome information that all of them raised young this season. Comparing this with the following statistics of Broley's regular area on the Gulf, one can readily see that nesting has been seriously curtailed.

In 1946, he banded one hundred and fifty birds in one hundred and five active nests. This season in the same area only sixteen of these nests produced any young. Broley banded only fifteen eaglets in eleven nests. He was unable to climb to the other five nests due to deep water in the cypress swamps, to late hatching or, as in two cases, because the old, dead trees looked so weak it would have been foolhardy to go up lest they fall and so bring death to the young.

These sixteen active nests do not give a true picture of the actual numbers of adult eagles in his territory. While sixteen pairs nested successfully, some forty-six pairs of adults failed to reproduce. In twelve nests the eggs were infertile or became addled but the other thirty-four pairs made no pretense of nesting. Here is where Broley has run up against a stone wall. Why have so many eagles loafed during the past four seasons?

It is true many were disturbed by the tremendous building activity along the coast but there were some nests, back in quiet places, that should have been in use.

There are many problems in nature that are still unsolved and this is one of them.

Broley found snakes quite plentiful this season. Recently, while following a narrow cow path through the palmettos, he spotted a big rattler coiled right in the path. Had he not noticed it, he would certainly have kicked it or stepped on it. As too often happens, he was not wearing his high "snake" boots.

The next day, when climbing up to a nest, he paused as his head touched the bottom of the nest. He heard a hiss and turning his head found that there was a large snake only twelve inches from his face. Fortunately it was a coachwhip and harmless. Apparently it had been living right in the interior of the high nest as three or four shed skins were interwoven through the sticks of the eyrie. Naturally the snake would be killed instantly by the parent eagles if it ventured up on top of the nest near the young. He could not tell what it had been living on but no doubt it would descend occasionally to catch mice, rats, and other rodents. We are told that snakes often go up into palm trees after rats. Friends have heard scuffling up among the big leaves and then have seen snake and rat tumble to earth.

On March first, while breaking a path through the thick

palmettos and vines to go in to band the young in the last nest before leaving for the north, he came across two beautiful king snakes, stretched out side by side. It was the first time he had seen snakes mating. They were still there an hour later when he was returning to his car.

Each winter in Florida Charlie spends some time taking new movies to be used in his lectures. Like so many other naturalists and photographers, he is continually trying to find something new to record. One day he was looking at the beautiful flag, flying wide over the water. "That's it," he decided, "I'll try to get a picture of the national emblem of the United States saluting the Stars and Stripes." It would mean considerable work and much time but it was worth trying. If he could get the two in the movie with no faking and no transposing, it would make a fine ending for one of his reels.

Mr. John Dolcater, genial President of the Chamber of Commerce, provided the flag pole. The nearest nest where such a shot would be possible was forty-five miles away in a large clearing, so he took the pole down there.

Frank Smith, a well-known Bradenton artist, helped Charlie set the pole up and they ran up a five-by-seven flag.

Then came the anxious period. Would the big bird fly anywhere near the flapping flag or would the sharp cracks it made frighten her too badly?

Luck was with the photographer! The eagle sailed gracefully over the starry banner and then returned again to tip its wing at the flag of the United States and the camera caught it all. Fortunately the lighting and color are perfect for even the sun gave good coöperation. Many readers of this will no doubt see this film at some future date. Although it only takes a minute to show it, a long time was needed to figure out just how to get the shot, how to arrange the pole, and quite a wait before the eagle came close enough.

This spring Mrs. Herbert R. Mills of St. Petersburg showed us a most unusual nest. An eagle will not allow another eagle to nest near the tree in which it has its eyrie. Usually they drive off any intruders that start building within a half mile of them. So, when Mrs. Mills said she could show us a nest of a Ward's heron within six feet of that of an eagle, we were intrigued. Moreover, both nests were in the same tree!

As we approached the great tree, gazing anxiously ahead we could glimpse the white head of the eagle as it sat on the nest and, sure enough, hardly six feet away the heron was standing on her nest of sticks watching us. There were four other heron nests within a hundred feet but only this one in the eagle tree.

Both movies and stills were taken of this unusual find, showing the heron on her nest and the eagle coming in to hers.

We wondered if the eagle might molest the baby herons. Certainly great horned owls would, but the eagle is not a vicious or cruel bird, and we are sure that they will tolerate these close neighbors and not cause any unpleasantness. Mother heron may even steal a surplus fish or so out of the other nest when her young are hatched and ravenous for food and the neighbors are off fishing.

We had to leave without finding out which eggs hatched

first and how things progressed. We hope to be kept informed, however, and learn just how well the two families got along. Just another of these surprises nature furnishes so often to keep her lovers interested and keen on taking field trips.

I will have my husband tell in his own words about a recent experience he had while taking movies of a very nervous eagle at her nest.

"I wished to get a close-up of the parent eagle sitting on a stub close to the nest containing one young bird. On a Monday afternoon I erected my blind on the ground, about thirty feet from the tree and left it there over night so that the eagle would gradually become accustomed to it.

"This blind was constructed with a light steel framework covered with green canvas and took only five minutes or so to set up.

"I slipped into the blind early Tuesday morning and placed my camera with a long telephoto lens in position. Fifteen minutes later one of the eagles came in from the Gulf and settled on the stub. Almost immediately it caught sight of my bright lens protruding from the blind and took off at once. Later she approached the nest but veered off again and I realized I was through for that day. I would get no coöperation from her unless I adopted other tactics.

"Wednesday morning I made an early start. Passing a fish market I noticed a cat near the door. 'Whose cat is that?' I asked.

" 'Yours if you want it,' the owner of the place replied.

"It was a stray, ready to be friendly so I took it along.

It followed me into the blind. Both adult eagles were off fishing and they did not see me enter the hide.

"Before long I saw one bird coming towards the nest and just as she was settling on the stub, I lifted the canvas a bit and tossed the cat out onto the soft sand.

"The eagle saw it immediately and forgot all about the lens. The cat sprinted back under the blind and again I gently threw it out. The eagle sat there entranced. What kind of an animal was this that erupted out of its den, upside down every time? I bet I threw that cat out sixteen times, and for half an hour the surprised eagle never moved and I made one of the best movies of an eagle that I have ever taken!

"Possibly cat lovers may take exception to this, but the cat was in no danger, being only a few feet from the blind. Apparently it did not resent my actions but seemed to think this was some sort of new game for it came back to me each time, rubbing itself against my foot, and purring contentedly, glad to get in out of the very hot sun.

"We returned to the fish market, still good friends."

CHAPTER TWENTY-FOUR

Banding Some Young Goshawks

PERHAPS THE fiercest of our hawks is the goshawk. His speed, power, and courage are phenomenal.

Charlie had gone scouting over in the woods on the main shore behind our island in Ontario one spring and, walking quietly along looking for the lovely lavender and white blooms of the lovely showy orchis, was startled indeed when a large hawk swooped directly at him. He sprang behind a tree to protect himself as well as to get a better look at the bird. After making sure it was a goshawk, he looked about for the nest since, although these birds usually nest much further north, he was sure from her actions that she had one near-by.

Sure enough it was some forty feet up in a hemlock and he rejoiced in the sight of his first one for this species. Getting a forked branch to ward off the angry parent, he moved over closer. Then the smaller male flew in and joined in the attacks and for some minutes Charlie was kept busy ducking as they tore in at him. At times he had to fall on his knees to avoid the raking talons.

[165]

Studying the tree, he saw that he could climb it so decided that when the young were a little older he would band them. As he left the pair kept after him until he was well away from that part of the woods.

That night he wrote to Dick Pough asking him to send up some bands so that he might put them on these birds. By return mail Dick wrote that he would bring up the bands as he wanted to be in on this.

We had paid a couple of visits to the nesting area, keeping a good distance away, so that Charlie could gauge the age of the babies, the distance to the nest and so forth. The hawks would attack viciously when we neared their section. I always had to promise to do just as I was told, to keep behind my husband and to duck when he told me. The red eyes of the birds fascinated me and I can assure you I was really frightened of them, their whole body is so streamlined that at the beginning of their dive towards you it blends perfectly with the background so that for a moment or so they are invisible. That moment is a terrifying one.

On the morning chosen for the banding Charlie gathered his equipment together. Although it was a warm day, he put on a heavy leather jacket, turning the collar up around his neck. He had taken a basket, formerly used for deep frying, put a wire mesh over this and tied it over his face. He had no way of protecting his head but, searching about in the woodshed, he found a discarded colander which was still sound. Deciding this would serve, he tied it firmly on his head. He was certainly a queer looking object but did not mind for he was determined to band these young goshawks.

Broley never uses gloves when climbing or banding but in this case he had to do so. We wanted pictures of the young as well as a close sight of them so he arranged to band them in a shelter on the ground. He wasn't sure he could manage to do it up in the tree with the old birds ripping at him.

I was not allowed to go very close but was placed under some brush where I could see but be safe from the birds. Dick went on a little further, then he too, took to cover. Alone, Charlie got his ladder up, fixed one end of a line he carries with him to a strong carton in which he planned to let down the young hawks and began his ascent.

All this time the parent birds had been swooping in at him like jets, their sirens going, "Kac, Kac, Kac" in a furious crescendo which grew in volume as he started up the tree.

The first time the female struck the colander on his head, she almost tore the stout rim off and must have hurt her foot but she struck again and again. Finding this had no effect on the queer looking object going towards her babies, she began on his leather coat and tore a huge chunk out of the back. His head had been hurt in spite of all the covering and we could see blood coming from it. We could see him flatten himself against the tree as she pounded him and I was glad when Dick called, "Come down, come down. She'll murder you."

My joy was premature. Charlie had no intention of descending without the young hawks. Ducking this way and that to try to evade the onslaughts, he continued on up and we wondered that he did not slip.

At the nest he was subjected to a more vicious attack if that were possible and he told us later that his head was ringing so from the blows on it that he couldn't hear the screaming of the parents. The little ones were quite docile and submitted quietly to being placed in the box. They were about four weeks old and downy white on the breast but already partly fledged with almost clove brown on the upper parts.

The box came down smoothly and Charlie descended the ladder buffeted by first one, then the other parent. At times both would rake him with powerful hind talons which seemed to clutch and tear as the bird passed over.

He brought the birds to the shelter and banded them. We took what pictures we wanted of them. Even through the heavy gloves Charlie's hands had been torn and now they were bleeding freely so that he had to be careful, putting the young back into the box, not to drip it on them. As he carried the box over to the tree, the parents who had retired to a high maple nearby dove at him again. At times the female would close her talon like a fist and smack him with it. He said it really hurt, though to watch his climbing steadily up, he gave the impression that all was going easily. Soon the box went up again and returned empty and I drew a sigh of relief when he got to the foot of the tree.

We were all quite excited, wishing we'd been able to take movies, exclaiming over the beauty and fierceness of this living blue lightning. Charlie, though was rather quiet.

"You know, Dick," he said at last, "that last band was pretty tight"—he had put on number sixes—"and those birds aren't fully grown. Those bands aren't the right size for them. They may cut into the leg. We'll have to do them all over again."

We groaned but he was right, of course. The bands were too tight. That night he and Dick cut down some Eagle bands and a few days later the whole thing had to be repeated. Again the goshawks struck and tore, screaming defiance although he had not hurt the babies before. These were rebanded and he got safely down again.

"I hope you never find another of their nests," I said for I had been really frightened by these birds.

He laughed and said, "Well, I'll look every year and try."

The goshawks have not been seen since in our vicinity. We have been told about a pair on a lake to the north of us and they might have moved there. We hope they have not been shot. It is true they help themselves to many a partridge, squirrel and if necessary, a hen or so but the sight of them should be sufficient payment.

The wings and slim body dart forward like a projectile seeming to proceed by some power outside themselves and the finely striped light underparts, dark crown bluish grey back blend so well into the background that at times, though right in front of you, the bird is not visible.

The goshawk deserves our praise for its fearless defense of its nest. It will attack again and again, even when shot at and, as an officer said when he had wounded one badly, "I never saw more vindictive fury expressed in a bird's eye than was shown by hers. She tried to attack me and would have done so had she not been so nearly dead, and unable to get at me."

Broley is glad indeed that the eagles do not treat him as the goshawks did. For several days his head ached from the blows, and the scratches on his back and any exposed flesh took some days to heal.

One of the young birds was shot that autumn near Cornwall, about a hundred miles away. Nothing has been heard of the other three so he hopes they are safe some place. He would be glad to band more of them if given the chance and hopes another pair may choose this section or that the same pair may return to gladden his heart with their swift sweep across lake or meadow.

CHAPTER TWENTY-FIVE

Home in Ontario

EARLY IN April, when his Florida banding is over, Charlie packs up his equipment and starts for his island home in Canada. There is always an argument when we begin loading as to which of us has the largest amount of unessentials to go into the packed car. True, we have the same sort of controversy at the end of October when we are planning the trip south but perhaps we do collect a few extras. It is an amicable argument for the most part and in the end he does manage to get everything in. Because he has about fifteen eagle's nests fairly near the Lake in Ontario he requires all extra ropes, ladders, bands and so forth in both places.

By the time we leave Tampa the days are hot and hibiscus, oleanders, jacaranda and other tropical shrubs and trees are all in bloom. As we travel along we go from this full summer into late spring in Georgia with its roses, wistaria and camellias to redbud and peach blossoms in the Carolinas, forsythia around Washington, or in a late spring cherry blossoms, until by the time we arrive at the international bridge it is winter again. We may even run into a snowstorm in northern Pennsylvania or New York.

[171]

Eagle Man

One spring we arrived at the little village of Delta to be met with the bad news that the Lake was still almost completely frozen over but that there was so much water near the shores, it would be impossible to get across. Charlie was daunted but he is never defeated. He got our local handyman to put a pair of sleigh runners under the boat. Then he rowed up the little creek, a beauty spot in summer but now desolate indeed with no sign of green on the bordering trees and bushes, down the open water to a point about a quarter of a mile from the cottage.

With a pike pole he got the boat up onto the ice then pushed it along by sticking the point in and shoving with all his strength. In places the ice was honeycombed so that the runners would not slide but he persisted and finally got across the ice, then got it into the water again for the short distance to the boathouse.

He had to make several trips in this way, then one Saturday evening the wind opened up a lead right across to the open water in front of the mainland. It was about ten feet wide so we decided that, as the next day was Easter—a very late one—we would all go to church in the morning. We got across alright but when we returned the wind had shifted and closed up the channel. By this time the ice had become much softer so that it would barely support the boat and yet was too hard to row through. With a north wind blowing a gale, an icy rain pelting at us we tugged and pushed the boat across. Jeanne was with us and I have never seen a more bedraggled party than we were when we finally reached the shore again.

Fortunately the wind changed that afternoon and by

morning the ice was practically all out so that further trips could be made easily.

Sitting in the warm cottage with the expanse of ice in front of us, it was enchanting to watch the gleaming black and white mergansers, both American and red-breasted, as they fished along the small openings or at the water's edge for alewives or shad. Their orange-red bills and feet looked as if newly painted and their white was such a contrast to the dirty-looking ice. Noisy flocks of gulls would join them or wheel over head. Some days an eagle or two would soar over in search of a fish. Almost as soon as the ice went out the mergansers left us, going further north.

Each year naturalists ask to be allowed to come up and visit us while Charlie bracelets his eaglets here. He used to do this in late May and early June but May is not a good month for visitors to come, so now he tries to drag the work out through June so that each group will see the birds in at least one nest checked and tagged. One eyrie is conveniently located up through the Narrows back of the cottage—a wonderful fishing district. While the trees are still leafless he can observe this nest, watching the parents and determining the age of the young by the way in which and the length of time the parent sits on the nest.

There are large islands on this lake which, when the trilliums are blooming, present a carpet of white. I am sure that nowhere else would one find larger, more beautiful plants and we are so glad that there are few people about to pick them.

The boundary of the lake, so gorgeous in autumn when the leaves of the maples flame red against the gold of the birch and the dark green of pines and cedars, is misted now with the most exquisite chartreuse. Daily we watch as the buds grow and unfold until all about is a wall of green in so many different tones, high-lighted here and there by the white of birch trunks.

Hiking in through fallen trees and last year's leaves to discover whether or not a nest is active, we have to step carefully over hepaticas and bloodroot, Dutchman's breeches and adder's tongue. These give place so quickly to violets—and such violets! Whole areas as blue as the sky. In other places we see mostly the lovely woods type with its white so delicately tinted with lavender. Yearly we search for trailing arbutus but have found no sign of it as yet.

All the eagle nests have to be checked at least once, so we try to do this as soon as possible. It is a happy moment for all when we see a parent on the nest or perched in a tree near by. This is not quite enough though. We must go close enough to make sure that the pair are really nesting, not just using this as a feeding station.

If, when we get close, the bird or birds fly right away and do not return, that eyrie is crossed off. There will be no banding there this spring. If they fly around us, scolding, we are happy for they are guarding young. Then an estimate must be made of the contents of the nest. If the parent was sitting low, only her head and a bit of her tail showing, she was covering eggs or very small young. Broley knows about the time to band so that a late nest may be left while the earlier ones are finished first.

Few of our guests have any desire to climb up once they

see the height. Occasionally one does go up, some start but come down after the first fifteen or so feet.

A stranger had asked to be allowed to take some pictures for a news reel and came with us to a very tall tree on an island in a nearby lake. He and his friends were slightly amused when Charlie asked him if he was in good condition.

"Why," he said, "I've done a lot of gliding. Besides, I'm just thirty and I understand you're nearly seventy. I guess if you can go up I can."

He negotiated the sixty feet to the first limb on the rope ladder but was white and shaken and said he felt sick. Charlie had gone up first but came down to where he was hanging to the limb and gave him a hand up to a spot where he could sit down to get his breath again. After a rest of twenty minutes or so he felt able to proceed and got up the other thirty feet to the nest. There were three young in this towering structure so Charlie took some close ups for him so that he'd be sure of them.

Coming down he lost his nerve completely and collapsed, falling the last six feet into the mud at the base of the tree, completely exhausted. He was a good sport, though, and when Charlie came down with the cameras and binoculars he said, "Well, sir, I take my hat off to you. I'd never have believed it." He felt Charlie's muscle, looked him over and then said, "Why you aren't even breathing hard. I guess you really are in good condition."

Although this district around Beverley Lake where we have our cottage has been settled for about a hundred and fifty years, there is still quite a bit of wild life around.

Throughout the season the lake is fished continuously and heavily but there are still large catches of Pike, Large and small mouthed bass with many really big ones. Best of all in Charlie's opinion there is still plenty of bird life and here he feels his eagles are holding their own.

Not many hobbies are so well adapted as this, fitting in perfectly with a life spent partly in the south and partly in the north. Charlie feels he chose wisely and very happily for himself. We are both grateful to Richard Pough who, as it were, talked him into becoming the eagle man.

If, he says, he has done anything to make people realize that the eagle is, like the people it represents and their country, courteous and forbearing but ready when necessary to put everything it has into the fight against aggression, he is happy. He claims it is ready to trust men and, secure in its strength, not too suspicious nor too ready to fight those who approach too near.

Like Dawson, he believes the dignity of a white-headed eagle should be more than a target for the envious and the murderer. We all honor it as a symbol. Let us honor it in life and see that others do the same.

APPENDIX

RETURNS: BANDING REPORTS

Recovered	Particulars		Where Banded in Florida
FLORIDA			
Bradenton	16 February '43	found dead	Bradenton	8 February '43
Bradenton	17 February '45	shot	Bradenton	23 March '44
Near Largo	29 March '39	found dead	Largo	28 January '39
Palma Sola	1 April '42	found wounded	Bradenton	26 January '42
Newberry	8 May '39	shot	Largo	4 March '39
Sumner	15 May '39	found injured	Largo	27 February '39
Tampa	19 May '44	found dead	Tampa	11 February '44
Tampa	20 May '39	killed	Gibsonton	12 February '39
Lakeland	1 November '44	found dying	Osprey	3 February '44
Sarasota	26 December '43	shot	Sarasota	2 February '42
Slater	28 January '46	?	Englewood	15 February '44
Graceville	2 December '46	shot	Placida	22 January '46
N. St. Petersburg	22 December '47	killed	Largo	11 March '47
St. Petersburg	26 April '48		St. Petersburg	10 January '47
Oxford	27 April '48	shot	Sarasota	18 February '47
St. Petersburg	5 April '49	tree fell	St. Petersburg	16 February '49
Ruskin	26 October '49	found dead	St. Petersburg	20 January '49
St. Petersburg	27 November '49	found dead	Tampa	9 February '48
Bonita Springs	June '49	could not fly	Fort Myers	31 January '49

RETURNS: BANDING REPORTS (*continued*)

Recovered	Particulars		Where Banded in Florida	
GEORGIA				
Statesboro	20 April '44	shot	Ruskin	29 January '44
Moniac	26 April '45	shot	Aripeka	23 February '45
Swainsboro	22 May '40	found dead	Crystal Beach	22 February '40
Hilltonia	7 May '41	shot	Placida	18 February '41
Alma	1 June '44	captured	Placida	15 February '44
Rentz	26 November '42	shot	Gibsonton	6 February '42
Canon	14 May '48	killed	Bradenton	6 February '48
Montezuma	2 October '48	shot	Placida	22 January '46
ARKANSAS				
Decatur	22 May '45	shot	Lutz	4 February '45
MISSISSIPPI				
Meridian	21 July '45	?	Fort Myers	13 February '45

RETURNS: BANDING REPORTS *(continued)*

Recovered	Particulars		Where Banded in Florida	
SOUTH CAROLINA				
White Pond	23 May '44	shot	Bradenton	23 March '44
Moncks Corner	29 July '43	found dead	St. Petersburg	19 January '43
Whitehall	7 December '43	found dead	Bradenton	10 February '43
Wando	1 August '45	wounded	Largo	19 February '45
Summerlow	3 June '46	found dead	Punta Gorda	12 February '45
Pinewood	26 April '48	shot	High Point	26 January '48
Myrtle Beach	14 June '48	verminous	Ruskin	23 March '48
Columbia	22 August '48	found dead	Fort Myers	25 February '48
NORTH CAROLINA				
Roxboro	8 May '41	captured	Placida	18 February '41
Fremont	11 May '43	captured	Englewood	17 February '41
Catawba	27 May '40	killed	New Port Richey	9 March '40
Creswell	29 July '40	killed	Largo	3 February '40
Wilkesboro	26 May '47	shot	Pine Island	29 January '47
Mocksville	8 May '48	?	Palm Harbor	2 February '48
KENTUCKY				
Elliston	20 May '47	shot	Indian Rocks	11 January '46

Recovered	Particulars		Where Banded in Florida
VIRGINIA			
Widewater	April '46	band found	Placida	20 January '46
Walnut Point	30 May '39	shot	Largo	4 March '39
Halifax County	8 May '46	shot	Boca Grande	3 March '46
Union Level	28 April '48	shot	Bay Pines	29 January '46
PENNSYLVANIA			
Ringtown	3 June '44	found dead	Sarasota	2 February '44
N. Springfield	29 July '44	found dead	Venice	18 February '44
Shawnee-on-Delaware	18 August '44	wounded	St. Petersburg	29 January '44
Clearfield	18 July '46	killed	Pine Island	22 January '46
Eaton Farm, Oaks	15 August '47	killed	Lake Butler	4 January '47
Waterfall	26 May '47	found dead	Ruskin	11 February '47
Leechburg	14 August '48	wounded	Sarasota	22 January '48
Huntingdon	26 August '49	shot	Englewood	28 January '47
OHIO			
Sandusky	19 September '45	found dead	Ozona	4 February '45
Crystal Rock	no date	broke neck on wire	St. Petersburg	24 January '45

Recovered	Particulars		Where Banded in Florida	
INDIANA				
New Castle	27 April '44	shot	Largo	1 February '44
ILLINOIS				
Homer	16 May '45	shot	Boca Grande	15 February '45
Mendota	30 August '43	shot	Englewood	16 February '43
MASSACHUSETTS				
Medford	25 May '48	found dead	Indian Rocks	13 February '48
CONNECTICUT				
Stonington	15 April '41	shot	Placida	18 February '41
NEW YORK				
Fort Terry	4 May '43	found dead	Ruskin	27 January '43
Columbiaville	8 May '39	shot	St. Petersburg	28 January '39
Pine City	21 May '45	shot	Largo	2 February '45
MICHIGAN				
Grass Lake	14 May '45	shot	Crystal Beach	24 February '45

RETURNS: BANDING REPORTS (*continued*)

Recovered	Particulars	Where Banded in Florida	
MINNESOTA			
Mora	17 May '49	found dead	St. Petersburg	9 February '49
MAINE			
Burnham	20 August '42	found dead	St. Petersburg	21 January '42
Round Pond	21 May '48	shot	High Point	26 January '48
QUEBEC			
St. Germaine	6 May '40	wounded	Indian Rocks	6 February '40
Lac St. Jean Co.	11 May '42	shot	Indian Rocks	22 January '42
St. Benoit	2 September '46	killed	St. Petersburg	24 January '45
NEW BRUNSWICK			
Leger Brook	23 May '42	shot	Tampa	25 February '42
Millbank	15 July '42	found dead	Bradenton	12 January '42
Chipman	20 August '44	shot	St. Petersburg	23 February '43
Maquaped Lake	?	shot	St. Petersburg	15 January '42
Coal Creek	10 June '48	shot	Englewood	25 February '48

RETURNS: BANDING REPORTS (*continued*)

Recovered	Particulars		Where Banded in Florida	
NOVA SCOTIA				
Halifax	10 June '44	found dead	Ruskin	25 February '44
E. Jeddore	24 June '44	shot	Tampa	21 February '44
Yarmouth Co.	19 September '42	shot	Ruskin	7 March '42
Halifax Co.	18 October '43	shot	St. Petersburg	23 February '43
PRINCE EDWARD ISLAND				
Kings County	1 June '41	shot	Largo	8 February '41
MANITOBA				
Lake Winnipeg	25 July '47	caught in trap	Placida	26 February '47

	1941 83 nests	1942 84 nests	1943 107 nests	1944 106 nests
Nests taken by Owls	11	4	6	5
Eggs taken by boys			1	1
Young taken by men	3			
Young killed by wildcat			1	
Young shot on nest		1		
Young died in nest				
Adult shot		1	2	
Adult killed by lightning	1			
Eggs failed to hatch	5	5	7	2
Disturbed during incubation			3	5
Nest blown down	1	3	1	3
Nest trees cut			7	4
Hurricane—the fall of 1944				
Lumbering				
Undetermined	4	4	5	6
No old birds returned to claim nest				
Birds around but did not nest				
Totals of nests lost	25	18	33	26
percentages	30%	21%	30%	24%

FLORIDA, 1941–1951

1945 115 nests	1946 124 nests	1947 123 nests	1948 112 nests	1949 108 nests	1950 92 nests	1951 82 nests	Totals 1136 nests
	5	7	6	3	7	7	61
			1	1			4
							3
							1
	2						3
	3						3
	6						9
							1
	6	29	30	31	19	15	149
			5				13
							9
		2	2	3	4	4	26
45							45
2							2
					3		22
		6	4	4	6	8	28
		7	9	23	30	28	97
47	22	51	57	66	69	62	476
40%	17%	42%	51%	62%	77%	78%	41.9%

APPENDIX

The Eagle as a Religious Symbol

MARTIAL AND religious symbols are so interwoven in the history of the Medes, Persians, Egyptians, and other races that it is hard to tell where one begins and the other leaves off. We know that many religious sects have seen in the eagle, if not a god, at least a messenger of the gods, the bearer of the souls of great ones to celestial bliss, and the embodiment of power and freedom.

This bird might indeed have been the Phoenix, that fabulous creature which was supposed to throw itself into the fire when it felt its energy waning and to have risen from the flames, fresh and virile again, and more beautiful than ever.

When depicted with the head of a lion it represented Ishtar, and was therefore a royal standard in Syria. It was connected with the sun as a symbol of omnipotence and virility. In other oriental countries it had this association also.

Very ancient drawings and carvings show the eagle with its head like a flame. Various devices are superimposed on the body to designate light, a deity, or the soul.

The Egyptians used the hawk in their religious symbolism, and we are inclined to believe that eagles were used also. The god Horus might well have had an eagle's head instead of that of a hawk, since the Assyrians represented one of their gods, Nisroch, with an eagle's head. Captive eagles were kept in the temples of the Hittites so that they might be used in various rites connected with the Phoenix, one reason why we think this might well have been an eagle.

Herodotus tells us that while the killing or destroying of any animal in Babylon was punishable by a fine, to kill an ibis or hawk—meaning also an eagle—meant death to the killer.

One cannot read Greek or Roman literature or history without realizing how very important the eagle was, especially on the royal standards. No banner was complete without its eagle on the staff; those of the emperor had eagles of gold and, though heavy, were carried proudly on high. They were the representation of the Roman god Jupiter or of his power, might, and independence.

For the Romans, death meant a journey to the realms of Olympus for an emperor since they considered these rulers to be divinities albeit a little lower in the scale than the other gods. Their bodies, according to custom, were burned on a huge funeral pyre. To the pile were added golden objects, costly jewelled ornaments, cloaks embroidered in gold and silver, wonderful hand-made mats, and other treasures.

After the great heap had been lighted and was well ablaze, a live eagle was released from the top, showing that the soul of the emperor was being borne on high to enjoy celestial bliss.

There is an ancient fable told on the clay tablets of Babylon in the cuneiform characters invented by the Sumerians. This tells about the reward given to a peasant by an eagle. The latter had devoured the young of a snake but the reptile, returning stealthily, seized the great bird. Though the eagle fought valiantly it was almost overcome by the serpent, which wound itself round about it, almost strangling it. A peasant, hearing the noise of the struggle, hurried up and, after slaying the snake, set the eagle free.

In gratitude the eagle told the peasant to seat himself on its back and then bore him to heaven so that he could dwell with the gods. Unfortunately, the gods did not desire to have him there but, loading him with treasure, sent him back to earth again. This may have been the origin of the myth of Ganymede who, because he was so beautiful, was, according to the Greeks, taken on the back of a mighty eagle to be cup-bearer to Zeus, chief of the gods.

When polytheism, or the doctrine of many gods, all having their own individual interests in worldly affairs, flourished, the constellation of Aquilla, the eagle, was thought to be the eagle god, watching at night over the world. On ancient tombs of this era will often be found the representation of an eagle with uplifted wings. This, to the archaeologist, signifies that the soul of the person whose name is on the tomb was supposed to have been carried to heaven by the eagle.

In Syria, the eagle was also the symbol of immortality and even on that most famous relic of early Christian art, the Great Chalice of Antioch, discovered with other treasures in Syria in 1910, we find beneath the representation of Our Lord as he looked, many believe, at the time of his death, a Roman eagle with wings fully spread, standing on a basket filled with bread meant for the sacrifice of the Mass.

There are no other records of the eagle in Christian art before the fourth century. This has been attributed to the fact that the Roman soldiers, for whom the eagle on their standards was their god, to which sacrifices were offered, and by which their most sacred oaths were ratified, cruelly persecuted or put to death any Christian they found. No doubt that would make the eagle a most detested symbol to this pitiful little group. It was not until after some two hundred and more years following the Crucifixion that this persecution ceased; it would have taken time for the Christians to forget how they loathed the symbolic eagle.

Jenghis Khan, the Mongolian chieftain, kept eagles in cages and had them taken along with his army. He is said to have believed more in might than in signs, so most of these may have been for use in hunting. To the soldiers, though, who were considered more terrible than those of Alexander the Great, they very likely represented power and sovereignty. It took a strong arm to hold the hooded eagle before he was loosed after his prey, but the Khan had that and how he must have delighted in the speed and ferocity of his bird, in its strength and courage.

That the eagle was used at all in the Mongolian religious ceremonies is not sure but certainly it was used and its actions studied for portents and omens. The Mongolians shared the belief of the Red man that certain animals had definite attributes and that the partaking of these or parts of them would give the eater an increase in the power, fierceness, speed, or whatever the attribute was. Needless to add, eagles were not killed for this purpose though certain other birds were.

Many of the Indian tribes have fables about chiefs or mighty warriors being borne aloft by the eagle to Gitchi Manitou, their greatest god. This bird still has a great importance in their rituals and tribal dances. It is a "Power" to them and they believed his feathers gave them swiftness, strength, and endurance. They did not kill eagles, however, but kept them alive in cages so they could take feathers as needed.

Amongst the southern tribes there was always one or more "catchers," men who were expert in capturing the mighty birds. They did not use traps for in that case the talons might have been bruised or crippled. Instead they dug a pit about a yard square and about two yards in depth near a large tree.

The catcher got into this hole and was covered over with branches of trees, leaves, sod, and grasses except for a small opening for his hand. The branches were fairly loose in one spot so that he could peer through there. When all was ready a dead rabbit was placed on top and a tame eagle was loosed there to decoy the wild ones. Then the assistants went away.

The soaring eagle, glimpsing the tame one, would alight in the tree and, after careful scrutiny of the area to see that there was no danger, would descend to share in the feast.

At once the concealed Indian grabbed it by the legs and, tearing apart the covering branches, dragged it into the pit. Here, because the space was too narrow to allow it to use its wide wings, the eagle was at a tremendous disadvantage, so the catcher would soon have it tied up, ready to be taken back to camp.

Often only a few feathers would be taken, then the bird would be freed again. If it was unable to fly due to the loss of its flight feathers, it was often tethered in the camp and fed until these grew in again.

Not only the feathers but the down also was used; and a treasured gift to friends, other chiefs, or people they wished to honour, was a small package of eagle down.

In connection with their tribal and religious rites, the Indians hold races. For some of these the runners come out with their black hair covered with eagle down and patches of it on brown shoulders and arms as well. As they emerge from their tents, onlookers throw more of the down into the air to add speed to the feet of their favorite runner. Almost every contestant will have an eagle feather in his hair and some wear one on the ankle as well.

The eagle dance, so beautiful when the dancer wears the great headdress and armlets of white-tipped feathers— which reach from shoulder to away past the finger tips— is copied from their idea of the flight of the eagle. Not many chiefs have enough feathers now to make this dance the spectacle it should be. True, they can and do buy plumage from Alaska, of birds which have been shot for the bounty. A poor Indian will often tramp miles along a transmission line, seeking a bird that has flown into the

wires and been killed. Feathers may sometimes be picked
up on the ground near a nesting tree. The Indian who finds
a dead eagle, while he mourns the loss of the fine creature,
will carefully remove all tail and flight feathers and down.
Feathers from a live bird are much preferred, as is the
down, since they last better and are more resilient.

In connection with the Eagle Dance, it is interesting to
note that last spring Broley was asked to get some flight pictures of a bald eagle so that when a movie is made up for
the Museum of Natural History in New York, showing
the Indian dance, a sequence of the bird may be shown for
comparison.

Before some of the races or dances, old men stroke the
muscular legs of the participants with an eagle feather. This
is to give speed and stamina to the runner. The feather used
often belongs to the young racer and may be one used by
some former champion. He will make sure, if this is so, to
reclaim it after the ordeal is over.

The captive eagles, kept in cages made of strong
branches, interwoven, are well fed and soon become quite
tame. Often, when they are only tethered on a long rope,
they chase the dogs and take their food from them. The
Indians treat them very much better than we treat some of
our poor captive birds.

To have a goodly supply of feathered headdresses, down,
quills, and so forth, gave a tribe standing and prestige. It
was ignominy, indeed, if they had to attend a tribal gathering with dilapidated war or rite bonnets or had only worn
and broken feathers to use in headbands or anklets.

The talons of the eagles were used for necklaces and

ornaments and were an important part of the medicine man's kit and regalia. Many of the totem poles in British Columbia have carvings of eagles on them. Designs of this bird on beaten copper, carved in bone, or worked in intricate needlework on leather, have been found in the burial hills of the mound-builders, those mysterious and early settlers. There are relics somewhat similar to these in some of the old tribes also. Some of the ornate tents used on special occasions have eagles worked or painted on them. A few such may be seen at the annual Stampede in Calgary, Alberta, at Banff in the summer, or at tribal meetings and dances in Western United States.

As far as is known the eagle was not used as a religious symbol in ceremonies in China or Japan. The dragon apparently took its place. Nor do we find anything about it in Hindu writing.

The belief that an eagle could gaze right into the sun came, possibly, from its early connection with that great orb during the period when the sun was worshipped. Certainly our expression of "an eagle eye" seems well chosen. These birds possess a very keen sight.

The Eagle as a Symbol of Might

FOR GENERATIONS the eagle has been used as a symbol by the mightiest nations. Not only has it been given the attributes of power, courage, freedom, and independence but it has been revered also as a messenger from the gods, the warden of Jove's thunderbolts.

Eagles were used on standards when the Persians swept all before them and Xenophon reports that an eagle of gold, with upraised wings, on a spear head always headed their army when they were on the march.

Astrologers studied very carefully the actions of eagles before any great event to learn the outcome. In Babylon, certain men of the nobility used the eagle as their seal when marking the clay tablets of the time that were used to ratify agreements or sales or even to mark their messages.

If, when starting on a raid or before, the army astrologer saw an eagle feeding on its prey, the raid would be lucky indeed. An eagle flying very high up also signified success, and in some cases a captive eagle was loosed just before the troops started off to make sure they would see such an augury.

An all-dark eagle meant trouble or disappointment, especially if the head was down, but one lighter in colour was a good omen.

The Romans used such portents, too, and bore their eagle banners proudly into battle. They felt that Jupiter accompanied them as these, his symbols, dashed on. This god was usually represented in their sculptures with his messenger, an eagle, at his feet.

According to Pliny, the great historian, a silver eagle with uplifted wings and holding a thunderbolt was adopted as the military standard in 104 B.C. This, on the end of a spear or staff, was to be carried at the head of every legion. Such was the order of Caius Marius for, he said, the eagle being ever first in battle should help keep them so.

During the Crusades, because men from so many different countries met together in their fight for the Holy Land, it became necessary to have some way of telling one group from another. Elaborate and colorful banners with unique designs were used for this and many countries claimed the eagle. In a number of cases a two-headed bird was used, especially on the standards of the Romans. Even the English had this; Edmund Plantagenet claimed a right to it since he had been elected a King of the Romans and he took it home with him.

Under Charlemagne the eagle standard waved over Italy and Germany. It was adapted there for seals as well as flags and was used on their money.

Russia took the eagle as its symbol around 1472 when it was claimed by Ivan the Great because he had married a niece of the last Emperor of Constantinople, who was descended from the Greek rulers. Ivan wanted to show that the Russian royal family belonged to this branch also.

Napoleon revived the eagle as a symbol and standard for France. When his little son, the King of Rome, was born, the citizens of Paris presented him with a very elaborate silver gilt cradle which had a small gold, imperial eagle at the foot. This child was often spoken of as L'Aiglon, or the Eaglet.

The Third Republic, in 1871, as if to banish forever from their country any signs of royalty, replaced the eagle with a laurel wreath.

The eagle of Germany was replaced in 1933 by the Swastika, and the eagle of Russia has given way to the red ensign with hammer and sickle.

Shortly after the Thirteen Colonies voted to declare their independence of Great Britain at the Second Continental Congress, meeting in the Pennsylvania State House, Independence Hall, in Philadelphia on July fourth, 1776, they realized they would need an official seal since, according to law and custom, grants and charters had to be sealed properly. Accordingly, a committee composed of Benjamin Franklin, John Adams, and Thomas Jefferson were given the task of drawing up the Declaration of Independence and choosing an emblem for the new country.

Of their first report, submitted on August 27th, the only part of the design to survive were the words, "E PLURIBUS UNUM" which had been suggested by Jefferson. Strangely enough, this motto contains thirteen letters, one for every state represented. It is not known whether or not this was intentional, but it seems reasonable to think so.

For over six years the choice was not settled, though countless debates and consultations were held and many devices submitted. A second and a third committee were appointed but their suggestions—two each—were not acceptable. The third committee, which had called in William Barton, a clever draughtsman with a knowledge of heraldry to help them, were the first to suggest an eagle. This was not the American eagle but one "displayed" as they say in heraldry. It was to be the "Symbol of Supreme Power and Authority signifying the Congress," and to sit atop a Doric column.

A second sketch was also sent in by Barton and these, with all the previous proposals, were given to Charles Thompson, Secretary of Congress, in June, 1782. He was asked to study them and then recommend what the proper choice should be.

In heraldry an eagle is "displayed" when both wings and talons are extended and the head is turned to one side, the observer's left. It is "close" when it shows in profile with the wings folded and it is "rising" when it stands with wings uplifted.

Secretary Thompson brought in his own design for the obverse side of the seal. He chose the American or bald eagle for the large, central figure, specifying that it should be shown "rising" and not "displayed." In place of the flag Barton had sketched in, the eagle now held a bundle of arrows in the left talon with an olive branch, instead of the sword and wreath of laurel, in its right.

The upper part or "crest" was a group of thirteen stars representing the states, surrounded by bright sunrays and clouds, and he arranged the red and white stripes in chevrons, one side of red and white, the opposite side of white and red. This shield was attached to the breast of the eagle and a scroll with the chosen motto was held in the bill.

The sketch was given to Barton who made a number of changes. He put in "pales," broad perpendicular stripes, on the escutcheon instead of chevrons, making them white and red alternating. Over this he put a blue chief.

He had the eagle "displayed" instead of "rising" and specified that the arrows should be thirteen in number. On June 20th, 1782 this design, having been considered appropriate, was formally adopted.

In Thompson's final report he explains his design at some length. "The Escutcheon," he writes, "is composed of the chief and pale, the two most honorable ordinaries. The pieces, paly, representing the Several States all joined in one solid compact entire, supporting a chief which unites the whole and represents Congress. The Motto alludes to this union.

"The pales in the arms are kept closely united by the chief and the chief depends on that Union and the strength resulting from it for its support, to denote the Confederacy of the United States of America and the preservation of their Union through Congress. The colors of the pales are those used in the flag of the United States of America; White signifies purity and innocence, Red hardness and valor and blue, the color of the chief, signifies vigilance, perseverence and justice. The Olive branch and arrows denote the power of peace and war which is exclusively vested in Congress. The Constellation denotes a New State taking its place and rank among sovereign powers. The Escutcheon is borne on the breast of an American Eagle without any other supporters to denote that the United States of America ought to rely on their own virtue.

"Reverse: The Pyramid signifies strength and duration—: the Eye over it and the motto allude to the many signal interpositions of Providence in favor of the American cause. The date underneath is that of the Declaration of Independence and the words under it signify the beginning of the New American Aera which commences from that date."

The American eagle was thus adopted as the emblem of the colonies on June 20th, 1782, and it became the symbolic representation of a new nation under a new government in a new world, a symbol of the American ideals of freedom. It became that of the United States under a constitutional government through the Constitution submitted to the Federal Convention in Philadelphia on September seventeenth 1787, which was put in force when Washington was inaugurated as President, at New York on September thirtieth, 1789.

The ratification by the Federal Convention of the Great Seal used under the Confederation was as that of the then government and provisions were made for its use and also its safekeeping.

New York was the first of the States to use the American eagle on its crest but now nine of the forty-eight states, Alabama, Arkansas, Illinois, Mississippi, New Mexico, Oregon, Pennsylvania, and Utah, as well as the Empire

State, use it on their armorial bearings in some part. It is used also on the seal of the Virgin Islands.

After the inauguration of Washington, Congress adjourned and a service was held in St. Paul's Chapel. Later an emblazoned and framed painting of the national arms and crest was ordered painted and suspended over the presidential pew in the chapel.

By 1841, the old seal die of 1782 had become very worn so a new one was ordered for both a negative and a positive die.

An engraver in Maryland was commissioned to do the work. He did not seem to realize that the design had to be followed exactly, in every line or shade of color since it had been enacted by law. Instead the die he produced, although it was accepted and used for forty-four years, was clearly illegal. The greatest error was in making the pales unequal, the red was twice the width of the white; and in having only six arrows instead of thirteen. Had the public known this there might have been a serious outcry for, were documents sealed with this spurious design legal?

In 1882, when the Great Seal medal was made by the Mint in Philadelphia to celebrate the hundredth anniversary of its adoption by the United States, the reverse side was cut for the first and only time. Contrary to general opinion, this was not because the design was considered mediocre as compared with the obverse but because there was no call for its use. Actually no reverse need have been chosen because the pendant seals, which required one, were becoming obsolete at the time this was designed. Now the seal is simply pressed down on a large wafer covered by paper which has its edges pointed. The hanging seals were inconvenient because it was customary, and almost necessary, to inclose them in elaborate boxes, often of silver or gold. The seal used on the Japanese Treaty after Commodore Perry's mission of 1854 was four and a half inches in diameter. It was enclosed in a golden box which was protected by a covering of velvet. The blue and silver cords which attached the wax seal to the document went into this box also. The whole thing, with the mahogany treaty case, cost about $2,500.00. It would be very much more today.

The pendant seal die for use on treaties was not cut until 1856. It weighed about twenty pounds and was almost eight inches in diameter. Its reverse side is blank. In 1869, the use of separate seals for treaties was discarded, and the regular seal, impressed on paper, is still in use.

In 1884, the Secretary of State, Theodore Frelinghuysen, requested Congress to prepare a third die so that all criticism of the illegal seal should be answered and it was recommended that obverse and reverse be cut at the same time.

The group called into consultation to decide on the design, under the able direction of Theodore Dwight, Chief of the Bureau of Rolls and Librarian of the Department of State, included the historian, Justin Windsor, Professor Charles Norton of Harvard, and the head designer for Tiffany's of New York, James Horton Whitehouse. This committee considered the design of the reverse from the angles of art as well as heraldry and agreed that it was very bad indeed. They decided that if it had been unused for a hundred years, it could be disregarded at this time also.

The Eagle as a Symbol of Might

The obverse was changed to have it more in accord with the tenets of heraldry, the chief changes being that the head of the bird now conforms more to that of the bald eagle, the tail is more realistic and the great wings curve up higher. Also, the talons are larger and the design shows more of them. Those in the other seal were very weak-looking for a bird that was supposed to be so strong.

However, the general description of the one enacted by Congress still fits. This great seal, which has been stamped upon every important public document issued by the Government of the United States and whose device is used also upon coins and paper money of the country, is probably one of the best known designs in the world at the present time and it is fitting that our splendid bird—the American bald eagle—should be so known, esteemed and loved.

The Eagle Used on American Money

MANY OF the most beautiful coins of the Greek and Roman eras have designs of eagles on them for, since the eagle was the messenger of the gods, these coins were often sent as omens or tokens as well as gifts.

On some of them the Greek letter D is thought to be the signature of that great artist Daedalus of Sicyon and like most of the others, shows a close observation of the bird as well as excellent craftsmanship.

In the Iliad we read that Zeus, king of the gods, sent to Agamemnon, as a special mark of favor, a coin or medallion showing an eagle bearing a fawn in its claws. This, a sign of victory in war, was more often shown with a hare rather than a fawn.

While these coins were used more as gifts or for transmitting certain messages, it is not surprising that, when the great new Republic of the United States of America decided to issue coins for legal tender, they should have chosen the eagle as a suitable representation to be put upon them.

The first representation of an eagle on any money of the United States was on a copper one-cent piece in 1776. This was issued in Massachusetts in that year. The eagle, standing with wings half spread on what looks like a crown is surrounded by thirteen stars. Strangely enough, this was before such an emblem appeared on the flag and may also have been before the signing of the Declaration of Independence. The other side shows a shield within a circle of stars.

On the New York one-cent piece of 1787, the eagle is more like the first design suggested for the seal of the country except that the head is turned to the opposite side.

The first American gold coins were minted in 1795 and were called eagles and half-eagles. These were ten- and five-dollar pieces. On both, the American eagle stands, wings extended, bearing a laurel wreath in its bill and carrying a palm branch. Later these were issued with an engraving much like that of the great seal but with the objects in the talons reversed. Quarter-eagles were minted in 1796 and double-eagles in 1849. These latter, worth twenty dollars, weighed five hundred and seventeen grains each, while the ten-dollar pieces, first minted, although they were about the same size, weighed two hundred and seventy grains each.

In 1849 gold dollars were issued, and in 1854, three-dollar pieces. These last, too often mistaken for the quarter-eagles worth two dollars and fifty cents, were soon withdrawn.

In 1794, the first silver dollar appeared and on it an eagle stands on a rock with wings extended; a wreath of laurel encircles all. That same year half-dollars, quarter-dollars and dimes were issued with a similar design.

In 1804, twenty thousand—a very goodly number at that time—silver dollars were struck for export to the Orient to compete with the Spanish dollar used there. The obverse of this coin had the word "Liberty" above a bust of that goddess and on the back was the eagle in heraldic pose, bearing in its beak a scroll on which was the motto "E pluribus unum." In the left talon was an olive branch while the right bore twelve arrows. Unfortunately almost the whole issue was lost when the ship on which they were loaded, bound for China, was lost at sea. Not more than eight of these are known to numismatists and they are collectors' items.

By the nineteenth century an eagle was almost always to be found on the coin money of the United States. Some of these birds have a snake in the talons, others stand on a globe of the world, and others on a shield, or carrying one.

In 1907, Augustus Saint-Gaudens did the very beautiful design now used on the fifty-cent piece. He also did the ones used for the ten-dollar gold coin, and the half- and quarter-eagles. His first mentioned design has been criticized as being more like the golden eagle than the bald. On it the splendid bird is standing on the fasces or rods which are the emblem of superior authority, and critics say that the tarsus appears to be feathered like that of the golden, instead of bare like that of the bald. Because birds walk or stand upon their toes, the long feathers above the shank seem to hang down and it is these rather than feathers on the tarsus that are represented.

The Eagle Used on American Money

Naturally the white head and tail, so distinctive of the American emblem, do not stand out on coins, which are all of one color. Neither will the bright yellow talons on the yellow legs show up to offset the feathers.

One of the most beautiful coins ever issued by the Government, and some people say by any country in spite of those beautiful coins of classical Greece and Rome, is the "double eagle" of Saint-Gaudens' design showing the bird in flight.

The law of the United States requires that on the gold and silver coinage of the country the figure or the representation of an eagle must appear. However, there is no specific type indicated nor any special pose; but undoubtedly it was intended that it should be the American bald eagle when the law was passed.

On the dollar bill the obverse and reverse of the great seal appear.

Mr. Edgar Wall, of Tampa, Florida, had in his office for the many years that he was postmaster there, a huge mounted bald eagle, the very bird from which the artist worked when he made his studies for the recent currency, coins, bonds, and official papers. When he retired from his post, Mr. Wall presented the historic bird to Southern College at Lakeland.

For a time, also, Mr. Wall had a most exquisitely carved eagle which, according to the legend in French on the yellowed paper pasted on the back, had been presented by the Marquis de Lafayette to his everlasting friend, his Excellency George Washington, as a symbol of a free America. It states also that Lafayette himself had designed it and had it carved in Paris. The wood is still beautiful though the faded handwriting is dated 1776, Washington.

Colonel Rudy de Barros, formerly of the French army, who achieved fame as a flier in 1925, when he made a solo airplane flight from France to Africa and then from Africa to the Azores, where he had to remain two weeks awaiting suitable weather before continuing to Brazil, had brought this in to Mr. Wall. He said his father, the late Marquis Emanuel de Moriere de Barros, formerly Brazilian Ambassador to the United States, Japan, and France, had found it in a second-hand dealer's shop in Paris in 1911, and had purchased it for five thousand dollars.

But how did it get back to Paris and when? Surely no one who knew the history would have sold it!